A TOUR TO THE LAKES IN
CUMBERLAND

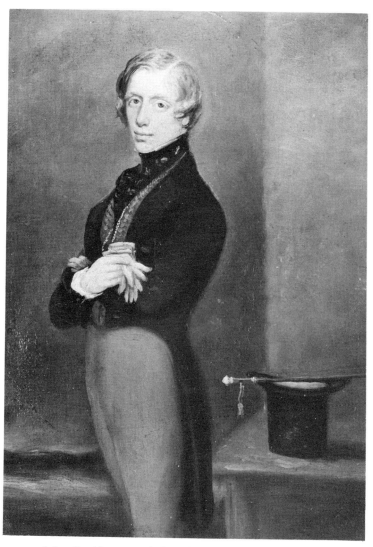

John Ruskin, portrait by Thomas Richmond. 1840–1.

A tour to the Lakes
in Cumberland

John Ruskin's Diary for 1830

Edited by
James S. Dearden

with an introduction by
Van Akin Burd

Scolar Press

Published by
SCOLAR PRESS
Gower Publishing Company Limited
Gower House
Croft Road
Aldershot
Hants GU11 3HR
England

Gower Publishing Company
Old Post Road
Brookfield
Vermont 05036
USA

British Library Cataloguing in Publication Data
Ruskin, John, *1819–1900*
    A tour to the lakes in Cumberland: John Ruskin's diary for 1830.
    1. English literature. Ruskin, John, 1819–1900.
    I. Title II. Dearden, James S. (James Shackley)
    828'.809

    ISBN 0-85967-812-1

Library of Congress Cataloging-in-Publication Data
Ruskin, John, 1819–1900.
    A tour to the lakes in Cumberland: John Ruskin's diary for 1830 / edited by James S. Dearden; with an introduction by Van A. Burd.
        p. cm.
    ISBN 0–85967–812–1
    1. Ruskin, John, 1819–1900–Diaries. 2. Ruskin, John, 1819–1900. . Journeys–England–Lake District. 3. Authors, English–19th century–Diaries. 4. Critics–Great Britain–Diaries. 5. Lake District (England)–Description and travel. 6. Cumberland (England)–Description and travel. I. Dearden, James S.
II. Title
PR5256.A34 1990
828'.803–dc20
[B]   89–70069
                CIP

To

my granddaughter

Caroline Jane Dearden Washington

Contents

Illustrations

Acknowledgements

For permission to publish the manuscript of the 1830 Diary I am indebted to the Trustees of the Pierpont Morgan Library, New York, owners of the manuscript, and Unwin Hyman Ltd, owners of the copyright on unpublished Ruskin material. I am grateful to both of these bodies for allowing this sole remaining unpublished Ruskin diary to be presented to the public.

I am also indebted to the Education Trust Ltd for the many references from manuscripts in the Ruskin Galleries, Bembridge School, Isle of Wight.

In connection with the editing of the manuscript I have received help or clarification on many points from many people – specialists in their own fields – who have generously given us the benefit of their knowledge. Particularly, I wish to thank Herbert Cahoon and Pamela White of the Pierpont Morgan Library; David Alston of the Graves Art Gallery, Sheffield; B. J. Ashwell, Architect to the Dean and Chapter of Gloucester; Patrick Baird of the Local Studies Department, Birmingham Public Libraries; F. H. P. Barker, Curator, Warwick Castle; D. J. Basnett of Gerrards Cross; Basil Bilton, formerly Curator of the Ruskin Museum, Coniston; Steven Blake of Cheltenham Art Gallery and Museum; The Revd M. F. Collier, Vicar of Hope; Peter Day, Librarian and Keeper of the Devonshire Collections, Chatsworth; M. J. Evans, Buckinghamshire County Archives Office; M. W. Farr, Warwickshire County Records Office; H. W. Fawcuss, Blenheim Palace; Dr Levi Fox of Shakespeare's Birthplace Trust, Stratford-on-Avon;

Charles Fyffe for his detailed knowledge of London; G. W. Nicholls of the Samuel Johnson Birthplace Museum, Lichfield; F. W. J. Scovil, Librarian, Magdalene College, Oxford; Miss Joan Sinar, Derbyshire Record Office; Miss Jill Sweetman of Merseyside Maritime Museum; John R. Wood of Cheltenham Public Library; Brian Woodall of Tideswell, Buxton; and Miss Joanna Woodall of Christ Church Picture Gallery, Oxford.

Help has also been received from the John Rylands University Library of Manchester; the Bodleian Library, Oxford; the Henry E. Huntington Library, San Marino, California, and thanks are due to the directors of these institutions.

I am particularly grateful to Adam Harris, at that time a prominent member of the Sixth Form at Bembridge School, who devoted much time to helping me check the transcript of the diary against the manuscript. The maps were specially drawn by Mr Alan Doe, head of the Geography Department at Bembridge School, and I am grateful to him for his help.

My principal debt of gratitude is owed to Van Akin Burd, Distinguished Professor of English (Emeritus), State University of New York, Cortland, New York. I first met Van Burd when he visited the Ruskin Galleries at Bembridge in 1960 in connection with his edition of *The Winnington Letters*. From that first meeting it has always been our wish to complete some joint Ruskin project. But time and distance have always intervened. In this project we have collaborated as fully as possible and I am deeply grateful for all the help and guidance which Professor Burd has offered. From the practical point of view a division of labour had to be devised; the task of editing the manuscript fell to me, and I thank Professor Burd for his provision of the Introduction.

James S. Dearden
Companion of the Guild of St George

Ruskin Galleries
Bembridge School
Isle of Wight

Introduction

Not long after Helen Gill Viljoen had carried to her home in Queens, New York, the extensive collection of John Ruskin's papers once owned by Frederick James Sharp of Barrow-in-Furness and given to her on his request after his death in June 1957, she resolved to edit the two unpublished diaries of Ruskin now in her possession. The first was Ruskin's diary of the tour to the Lakes with his family in 1830 when he was eleven years old, the subject of the present volume; and the second the large ledger containing his diary entries from 1873 into 1881 and during 1883 and 1884, the work which she subsequently published as *The Brantwood Diary of John Ruskin* (New Haven: Yale University Press, 1971). Her original intention had been to include the two diaries in a single volume, but by 1968 she had decided they were so unrelated it would be better to publish separately the record of 1830, 'the last of Ruskin's as yet unpublished diaries.'[1] On her death in 1974 she bequeathed to me the few pages of her notes for an Introduction to the diary and her transcript of Ruskin's text.

I could argue that what Ruskin calls the third Fors, that element of happy chance in life, has been at work in the choice of James S. Dearden for the task of editing this diary. He was appointed Curator of the Ruskin Galleries at Bembridge School, near Bembridge in the Isle of Wight in 1957, and became acquainted with Viljoen during her study at Bembridge in 1959. He had exchanged many letters with her about the course of her work on the diaries and often furnished her with information from the Ruskin collection at Bembridge, which had been assembled by the educator and founder of the school, John Howard Whitehouse (1873–1955). Dearden, a native of Barrow-in-Furness and later a boy at Bembridge School, had known F.J. Sharp and recalls having first seen the 1830 diary in Sharp's rooms about 1946. His interest in studying it dates to late 1959 when he was writing an essay on Ruskin's visits to the Lake District as a 'tourist' before he moved to Coniston, making nearby Brantwood his home in 1872.[2] By 1968 Dearden was at work on an edition of *Iteriad* (Newcastle upon Tyne: Graham, 1969), Ruskin's versification of part of the travels described in his diary of 1830, which the boy began a little more than three months after the return of the family to London. For this work Viljoen loaned Dearden a transcript of the diary from which he included several brief citations in his notes to *Iteriad*. He also drew help from his personal collection of rare books and prints on the Lakes, as well as his own retracing of the route of the Ruskins – sources which he uses again here. Dearden meanwhile was establishing his stature both as an editor, publishing *The Professor: Arthur Severn's Memoir of John Ruskin* (London: Allen & Unwin, 1967), and as a writer, as shown in his *Facets of Ruskin* (London: Skilton, 1970). In connection with his editorship of *The Ruskin Newsletter* since 1969, he has gained pre-eminence for his numerous bibliographic studies. He is at present editing the forthcoming Soho bibliography of Ruskin. It is a rare annual Victorian bibliography that does not list Dearden among that year's contributors to Ruskin scholarship.

Publication of the diary of 1830 has had to await the pleasure of the second Fors, the portress who requires patience of those at her gate. The diary was preserved by Ruskin's parents among the other notebooks of his juvenilia, and was later kept at Brantwood. Ruskin made his only known reference to it in his autobiography *Praeterita* in 1885, in a passage omitted from the final version. 'There once existed, and may somewhere yet, a piece of joint diary by Mary and me, supplemented occasionally – which was the greatest of favours and encouragements to us – by a word or two by my father.'[3] When W. G. Collingwood collected and edited Ruskin's poems in 1891, he listed and numbered the early Ruskin manuscripts at Brantwood. His No. X was a 'cover' containing several manuscripts, the first of which was the diary of 1830. Because the manuscript does not indicate its authorship but is written in the alternate handwriting of Ruskin and his cousin Mary Richardson, Collingwood may have had in mind Ruskin's reference to the diary, or he may have consulted Ruskin himself who was then in failing health at Brantwood, when he assigned joint authorship to it in his description: '(a.) "Journal [by John Ruskin and Mary Richardson] of a Tour to the Lakes in 1830;" in two paper books = 44 + 20 pages.'[4]

By 1903 steps had been taken to improve the preservation of these paper books as Ruskin's editors, E. T. Cook and Alexander Wedderburn, observed that year in their second volume of the Library Edition of Ruskin's works. Repeating Collingwood's listing of the early manuscripts they added that the diary of 1830 'is now separately bound, two leaves of the original, presented to the Ruskin Museum at Coniston by Mrs Severn, being replaced by a copy of them.'[5] The editors had also prepared a working transcript of the diary which Wedderburn later would bequeath to the Bodleian Library.[6] The diary, as we see it today at the Pierpont Morgan Library, consists of the two paper books of different sizes bound together in red buckram, lettered in gilt: *Ruskin MS, Tour to the Lakes, 1830*. Measuring 8⅛ by 8½ inches, the volume is very slightly larger than the first paper book (9 by 7 inches), which consists of 44 pages. The sheets in the first paper book are watermarked 'G. Wilmot / 1830', and are impressed in the upper left corner with a stationer's stamp of an embossed crown which appears to have been applied to the quire of paper as the impression becomes fainter on successive sheets. The second paper book measures 8 by 6¼ inches and consists of 20 pages with all but the outside sheet watermarked 'I & J Dewdney / 1826'. The two leaves which Cook and Wedderburn noted as having been presented to the Ruskin Museum at Coniston are in fact the outside folded sheet of the second paper book, comprising pages 45–6 and 63–4. These pages were replaced in the manuscript by a careful line for line transcript made by Collingwood, as authenticated along the inner margin of page 45 in a note by Sharp: '. . . The writing, on the pages substituted in this book, is in the hand of W. G. Collingwood. (F. J. Sharp)'. Mrs. Arthur Severn, Ruskin's cousin and heir, had presented the pages to the museum because on page 45 they contain Ruskin's first description of Coniston. It is not clear when she gave the pages to the museum (in whose ownership they remain) but most likely she did so when the newly built museum was opened in August 1901. Because the sheet of Collingwood's transcript is bound into the volume with the rest of the manuscript, the binding must date between the time of her gift and 1903. All the pages of the bound manuscript have been numbered in pencil, probably just before the sheets were sent to the binder. The pages on the substitute sheet are unnumbered. I shall comment later on the role of Mary Richardson in this manuscript.

If they could have secured access to it, Joan Evans and John Howard

Whitehouse would have included the diary of 1830 in their edition of Ruskin's diaries, the first volume of which appeared in 1956.[7] Before the sales of Ruskin's papers from Brantwood in 1930 and 1931, somehow this diary had become separated both from the juvenilia where Collingwood had listed it as part of No. X, and from the set of Ruskin's diaries as Cook listed them in 1909 in his Catalogue of the Ruskin manuscripts, where the diary of 1830 begins the list.[8] Only Items I–IX of the juvenilia comprised Lot 112, i–vi, as described in the sales catalogue, *Manuscripts and Remaining Library from Brantwood*, prepared for the auction at Sotheby's on 24 July 1930. The Ruskin diaries comprised Lot 111, as shown in this catalogue, but missing from the set were the diaries of 1830, the later one now known as *The Brantwood Diary*, and a third volume in which Ruskin's father, John James, had originally written his list of family tours. The buyer of Lot 111 was Whitehouse, who later was dismayed to learn that he did not have all of the diaries. The sale at Sotheby's on 18 May 1931 contained as Lot 32 five notebooks including the missing volume that originally had been John James's, which Whitehouse was able to secure. Lot 27 in the same sale comprised several of the manuscripts once included within the 'cover' in Collingwood's Item X, but not the diary of 1830. The missing volumes next appeared in the collection of F. J. Sharp, an obscure disciple of Ruskin who, like Whitehouse, had become interested in him in his youth. Self-educated and a teacher of carpentry, Sharp also began collecting Ruskin manuscripts and drawings at the time of the sales. In the absence of other evidence we may conjecture that he purchased the 1830 diary from the Grasmere dealer T. H. Telford who had bought extensively at the final three-day auction held in the garden of Brantwood in July 1931.

In the summer of 1947, Whitehouse had become acquainted with Sharp through the young Dearden. Knowing of their common interest in Ruskin, Dearden had arranged for Whitehouse to visit Sharp on his way back to Bembridge after a trip to Coniston. It must have been a great moment for Sharp to receive in the modest house where he was only a lodger so eminent an educator and scholar whose earlier career had included nearly a decade of service as a member of Parliament. Now in his mid-seventies, Whitehouse headed a school distinguished for its designs to carry out many of Ruskin's ideas on education. Dearden recalls Whitehouse's growing astonishment as Sharp brought out the treasures of his collection. When he produced the two diaries, Whitehouse (so Dearden recalls) exclaimed, '*I* bought the diaries, so how do you come to have them?' Deaf to any offers for his collection,

Sharp quarrelled with Whitehouse in 1950 when the latter, through an oversight, failed to acknowledge Sharp's loan of some letters for inclusion in Whitehouse's *Vindication of Ruskin* (London: Allen & Unwin, 1950). Determined not to make any further loans to the rival collector, Sharp refused Whitehouse's request to include the diaries in the edition which he and Evans were projecting.

The diary of 1830 remained first in the Sharp collection, then in Viljoen's possession until her death when she bequeathed it to the Morgan Library. Through these changes of ownership in private hands, the diary has been seldom cited: first by Collingwood who included four passages from it in his notes to his edition of Ruskin's poems; again in his biography of Ruskin where he summarizes the diary;[9] and by Cook in the second volume of the *Library Edition* where he uses Collingwood's notes to the poems, adding two more citations.[10] For the same reasons the diary was not exhibited until 1965 when Viljoen displayed it in her exhibition of the Sharp Collection at Queen's College, New York. In July 1977 the Morgan Library also included the diary in its exhibition of the Viljoen bequest, the volume being opened at Ruskin's account of the visit to Gloucester.

*   *   *

In his *Iteriad* Ruskin chose to versify only the three weeks in the Lake District included in the family summer tour of 1830. The diary records the three months of the Ruskins' travels from their departure from London on 18 May to their leaving Cheltenham on 17 August, from whence they returned by way of Oxford and Langley, arriving home about 19 August. Besides the account of the visit to the Lakes, the diary contains other passages of considerable interest such as the description of Ruskin's first visit to Oxford, his exploration of the caverns of Derbyshire, his visits to great houses along the route, and to cathedrals – notably that of Gloucester. 'It is of the essence that in this first part of all his diaries we should find Ruskin recording facts and impressions which remained basic to his creativity, and vision, throughout his life,' Viljoen observes in her notes to me on this diary. The whole trip, and especially the time he spent in Derbyshire – 'a lovely child's alphabet; an alluring first lesson in all that's admirable chiefly in the way it engages and fixes the attention,' so he wrote later of this countryside[11] – was richly fruitful for his future work.

This was the fourth of the young Ruskin's visits to the Lakes. During the summers his father took his annual holiday from the firm of which

he was a partner – Ruskin, Telford, and Domecq, the London agents
for the wines of Pedro Domecq of Jerez, Spain. Henry Telford who had
furnished the capital for the business would manage the counting-
house during his junior partner's absence, usually a period of two
months, the responsibility which John James Ruskin carried the rest of
the year along with most of the travel for orders of wine. The holiday,
as Ruskin recalls in *Praeterita*, ordinarily began about the fifteenth of
May, a few days after the family observance of John James's birthday
on the tenth. For these posting tours Telford usually would lend his
own travelling chariot, luxurious for two, as Ruskin recalls, with
himself as a boy seated between his parents but forward on the small,
cushioned box containing his clothes. Because Telford's chariot lacked
a driver's seat the boy enjoyed an unobstructed view through the four
windows which formed 'one large moving oriel, out of which one saw
the country round, to the full half of the horizon'. The 'dickey', the
outside rear seat of Telford's chariot, was wide enough for two, Ruskin
writes, and here rode John's nurse Anne Strachan who had entered the
service of the Ruskin household in 1814 when she was a child of
fifteen, and occasionally John James 'when the scenery and day were
fine'. The chariot in Plate 2, though fitted with a driver's seat, appears
otherwise very similar to Telford's. The family journeys included visits
to sherry customers and, if northward, to Perth where they stayed with
Ruskin's favourite Aunt 'Jessie', the sister of John James and widowed
wife of Patrick Richardson.[12]

Riding on a fine day from Warwick to Coventry in February 1822,
during a visit to his customers in this vicinity, John James wrote to his
wife that he must take her there. 'Either I have so associated all that
neighbourhood with Midsummer Nights Dream or else there is some
peculiar beauty in the Country which produces a wonderful effect on
Beholders . . . I hope to view it all with my Love some summers day.'[13]
According to Ruskin's memory of this holiday, they took passage by
boat to Scotland[14] and returned by the Cumberland hills among which,
he later declared to the painter Samuel Prout, 'I was born *again*, at
three years old'.[15] They probably travelled through the Warwick
countryside as they came south, including a visit to the ruins of
Kenilworth in which John James, as a great reader of Scott, had also
expressed an interest earlier that year. Ruskin, thinking of that
summer's tour or the next visit to the Lakes in 1824 when they visited
Coniston and spent a few days at Keswick, wrote in *Modern Painters* III
(1856) that the first thing he could remember as an event in his life 'was
being taken by my nurse to the brow of Friar's Crag on Derwent Water;

the intense joy, mingled with awe, that I had in looking through the hollows in the mossy roots, over the crag, into the dark lake, has associated itself more or less with all twining roots of trees ever since.'[16]

Poor profits in 1826 made it necessary for John James to do more than his usual amount of travelling among his customers, and he apparently delayed his holiday until late summer. 'This will be a barren year . . . for my only House at Yarmouth had not touched a Cask of last years Importation', he had written his wife in March of that year.[17] He could not be at home even for his birthday.[18] In Scotland that September, John who by now had begun his versifying, wrote of the autumnal lights on the River Earn 'precious for its shining drops'.[19] Passing through the Lakes on the way to or from Perth, the family travelled by way of Coniston and Keswick, the boy recapturing in his memory the cliffs of Skiddaw and the 'looking-glass' of Derwentwater which he would describe in the poem written in the spring months of 1829 for his father's birthday of that year.[20] John James, looking back over this holiday of 1826, would recall it for his wife as 'our delightful Journey together'.[21]

The Ruskins, according to Collingwood, had arranged 'a great tour' through the Lakes for 1828,[22] but the death of Jessie Richardson in May obliged them to cancel their plans. In the West Country apparently for some preliminary business calls they heard the news in Plymouth on 24 May where the young Ruskin for the first time saw his father 'in deep distress of sobbing tears'.[23] John James, now committed to looking after the four surviving children of his sister, invited Mary Richardson, the only girl, to live with them. Adopting her as a member of the family, he told his friend George Gray in Perth that Mary would be brought to London about 15 July when they expected to return home.[24] Their route back to London took the family through Stratford-on-Avon where on 3 June, so Dearden has discovered, 'John Ruskin' and 'Mr & Mrs Ruskin' signed the Visitors' Book at Shakespeare's birthplace.[25]

Mary Richardson was to remain in the Ruskin household for nineteen years until she married Parker Bolding. She died in 1849, only two years later. She was four years older than John, who recalls her as

> a rather pretty, blue-eyed, clumsily-made girl, very amiable and affectionate in a quiet way, with no parts, but good sense and good principle. She became a serene additional neutral tint in the household harmony. . . . When we travelled she took somewhat of a governess position towards me, we being allowed to explore places together without my nurse; – but we generally took

old Anne too for better company.

She became a great companion for Mrs Ruskin, the sadness of Mary's orphanhood touching her with feelings she could not conceal in her treatment of her niece and son.[26] Mary, accustomed to living with brothers, could challenge John, telling him on one occasion that his letters to his father were 'nonsense enough'.[27]

The addition of Mary to the modest Ruskin home at 28 Herne Hill in Dulwich may have persuaded John James that this summer holiday of 1830 would be a good time to make some extension to the house, together with interior improvements, particularly in the children's rooms. Since 1823, when the Ruskins moved to Herne Hill, they had been renting the house, and only in 1829 had they purchased the remaining lease.[28] Greater profits from the wine business had made these changes possible. In 1829 the partners held second place among the merchants exporting sherries from Jerez; in 1830, they headed the list, and John James's profits stood at their highest level since he had entered the business.[29] Sales may have increased because of the presence of Pedro Domecq who had come over from Spain to join John James during the last months of 1829 on his visits to his customers. It had been a good year for the Spanish wines, Domecq having 'the most magnificent Stock of wines perhaps at this time in Existence', so John James wrote to George Gray.[30] This prosperity, the alterations to the house, and Mrs Ruskin's growing concern about her husband's health apparently led John James to extend his holiday from two to three months to carry out the tour of the Lakes he had planned two years earlier. Precautions for her husband's health had been a theme in Mrs Ruskin's letters of 1829. As they came to plan the tour of 1830, she wrote to him that she thought this journey would improve his health.[31] A nephew of John James whom the latter had set up as a wine merchant in Glasgow informed George Gray on 28 May 1830 that he had heard recently from London that 'Uncle Aunt, Mary & John are Travelling throughout England, on acct of Uncle & John's health, they left London on 18th May.'[32] The decision to extend the holiday was wise. By mid-August 1830, it appeared that the work on their house would not be finished by the time of their scheduled return. 'We have been wanderers for three months without House or Home & I fear it will be October before we are again settled at Herne Hill, little as there was to do to the House they are sure to make that little long,' John James laments in a letter written from Cheltenham on 1[4] August to a family friend, Sarah Corlass of Hull.[33]

It was in the autumn of 1829 that John James must have written to his wife proposing that they undertake this tour the next summer. His letter is missing but in her reply Mrs Ruskin wrote that she looked forward to this journey with 'unspeakable delight. John quite danced for joy when I told him you intended taking us with you to the Lakes.'[34] John also must have written to tell his father how eagerly he looked forward to the tour. John James, replying from Chester on 26 October, told his son: 'You can Scarcely be happier at the thoughts of going to the Lakes with me than I am at the Thoughts of going to the Lakes with you. I miss your company prodigious.'[35] Preparations were made. John James's account book shows that on his birthday, 10 May 1830, he bought 'Colours [for] John', perhaps a new paint box for his son to take on the tour. Four days later he bought himself a 'Dressing Box £6' and 'Razors 31/-'.[36] All in readiness, the family – Mr and Mrs Ruskin, John, Mary Richardson, and very likely nurse Anne (although she goes unmentioned in the diary) – left Herne Hill, as the diary shows, at seven on Tuesday morning. If they used Telford's chariot, as seems probable, Mary could have joined Anne outside on the dickey.

The diary and *Iteriad* reveal the family's pattern of travel which became fixed, Ruskin recalls in *Praeterita*, as that of their home life.[37] Seven o'clock was their customary time for departure. In his verses Ruskin describes the early morning bustle at the inn attendant on their leaving:

> At length the time came, when, the bill being made, –
> Boots, hostler, and chambermaid all duly paid, –
> Sticks, bonnets, hats, greatcoats, all duly prepared, –
> Our elegant carriage rolled out of the yard![38]

Ordinarily they would travel a stage before breakfast. Leaving Preston at the usual hour on 14 July, for example, they drove ten miles before breakfasting at an inn at Yarrow Bridge. They would arrive at their destination by late afternoon – at four o'clock when they arrived at Oxford – and have dinner before walking about in the long evenings. During the day they would visit the local sites of interest, often seeking the best spot for enjoying a particular prospect. They would not travel on Sundays, but save the mornings for church and the afternoons for local walks. Choosing the best inns for the tour, John James was prepared to travel in style, entering in his account book at the end of the year £422 as the cost of their holiday.

* * *

Since the only date mentioned in the manuscript comes at the beginning, Dearden establishes the calendar of the tour primarily according to the timetable of the diary and *Iteriad*, using such clues as Ruskin's 'to morrow' or 'next day' or occasional references to the day of the week. The account is indefinite at some points as to how long the party stayed in a particular place, but the knowledge that the Ruskins habitually did not travel on Sundays helps to pin-point certain dates of arrival or departure. First among the external sources which also have been of aid on dates is again the letter from John James to Miss Corlass of Hull in which he makes the only known contemporary reference to the diary: 'Of our journey I must not say much for Mary & John have kept a Journal which I suppose you will see.'[39] Fortunately in 1830 Ruskin was a keen signer of Visitors' Books. Two that have been located confirm the presence of the family in Stratford-on-Avon on 25 May and at Chatsworth on 11 June.[40]

Ruskin's specified 'fortnight at Matlock' on their return journey may appear vague, but fourteen nights from their known arrival date on 19 July carries him past Sunday to Monday morning, 2 August, when they decide to avoid Evesham for a change of horses because an election was in progress between the second and fourth of that month.[41] John James's unpublished correspondence with George Gray corroborates his presence in Matlock on 20 July, and in Cheltenham on 4 August.[42] The arrival of the party in the latter town, moreover, was reported in the *Cheltenham Journal* of 9 August. Since this was a weekly paper published on a Monday, they would have appeared in this health resort during the preceding week. Tuesday 3 August, is the likely day of their arrival with departure on Tuesday 17 August, the period which Ruskin specifies in his diary: 'We remained here for a fortnight. . . .' John James in his letter to Miss Corlass of 1[4] August says that they 'are only 10 days here & go on Tuesday to Mr DePrees[,] Langley near Windsor'. The diary omits the timetable of the Ruskins' return to London, but an itinerary left by John James indicates that the route was by Oxford and Langley where they were to visit the family of Charles T. DePree, one of whose daughters had attended Mrs Ruskin during her confinement with John.[43] If they completed their return without any lengthy stays, as seems likely, they would have arrived home about 19 August, the end of the three month term of absence for which John James may have bargained with Telford. Whether John James's fears were realized that Herne Hill would not be ready to receive them is not known, but on 28 August he was writing to George Gray from London.[44]

The chief problem in establishing the itinerary arises in the manuscript at the top of page 29 where Ruskin in the midst of his account of their stay in the Lakes, breaks the narrative of their drive from Keswick to Patterdale on 1 July with an account of their exploration of Peake Cavern near the village of Castleton in Derbyshire which did not take place until 16 July. From page 29 to line 5 on page 38 the diary relates their adventures during the four days they stayed in the neighbourhood of Castleton, until they 'set off' for Matlock on 19 July. A short line was drawn below this last entry, followed by resumption of the drive to Patterdale. The account of the journey continues both geographically and chronologically until at the head of page 52 it comes to the end of the drive from Chapel-en-le-Frith to Coniston, with the words, 'see page [29]',[45] thus marking the point at which the Castleton episode should have appeared. Where the Castleton episode ends on page 38 with the words, '. . . we immediately set off for Matlock', the narrative continues on page 52, following the page reference, with 'We intended dining at Bakewell which is about 10 miles from Matlock. . . .'

Early in their correspondence Viljoen and Dearden had identified this problem in the manuscript, and Dearden has worked out a convincing explanation for this thrusting of the visit to Castleton into the events of their travels in the Lake District. The diary of 1830 differs from the bulk of Ruskin's other diaries, first because it is in the handwriting of both Ruskin and Mary Richardson, and second because it was not written daily, but apparently at a late stage of the tour. John James's penchant for keeping a diary of his travels may have led him to keep one of this tour, although no such diary is now known to exist, and his son, who was writing poems along the way, may also have kept notes on their adventures as he had done in 1828 when he accompanied his father on a visit to the Isle of Wight.[46] The peculiarities of the arrangement of the text suggest that this diary was composed during the holiday itself probably with help from notes of both father and son, at the suggestion of the parents or John perhaps to keep the children occupied when they were not otherwise busy.

The chronology of the tour shows two stays of a fortnight each at Matlock between 19 July and 2 August, and at Cheltenham between 3 and 17 August, the latter a centre from which John James often called on his sherry customers. These two long visits may have been intended to fill up time while the builders finished their work at Herne Hill, or, if the tour was undertaken in part for the health of John James and his son, to enable them to take the waters at these two resorts well-known for their mineral springs.[47] Since the family had already spent several days at Matlock on their way to the Lakes, the return visit may have been tiresome, and Ruskin records only a few days' visit by a friend, a journey to Bakewell, and second visits to Chatsworth and Haddon Hall. Indeed, as Ruskin asserts in the diary, they had already seen 'all the principal places and things, and as the weather was so excessively warm that we could not go out in the evening, we saw nothing new'.

This may have been the point when the young Ruskin improved his notes on the tour, beginning with those exciting events at Castleton which were freshest in his mind, especially the 'rapture' (as he calls it later)[48] of the family's exploration of three caves by eerie candlelight. As he would do later with *Iteriad*, we may conjecture that he first made a rough draft of these four days which he and his cousin then copied into a home-made book planned for the journey as a whole. From the time he was seven years old the boy had delighted in making these 'books' of plain paper. Now, picking up 11 folded sheets inserted into each other to form a quire of 44 pages, Ruskin saves the first 28 pages for the account of the earlier part of their tour which he will write later. The children may have resolved to have a game of taking turns in copying into this book what Ruskin had written, one of them sometimes stopping in mid-sentence as on page 3 of the manuscript (Plate 1), for the other to take up the task. It is not surprising that the young author seized the lion's share of the work in the ten pages occupied by the account of the adventures at Castleton, allowing his cousin to copy only three relatively short and less exciting passages. The care of the handwriting suggests that the children intended this to be their fair copy, but their work was soon marred by necessary deletions and interlinear insertions particularly in the work of the younger copyist. It is also evident, as Ruskin said, that John James read through the manuscript to supply 'a word or two', in one place a word omitted from a passage in his son's hand.

At Matlock Ruskin may have continued his writing, or again we may conjecture that he used the long fortnight at Cheltenham where indeed he finished it, since the diary does not proceed beyond that point. Their stay in Cheltenham was enlivened by an evening of fireworks which Ruskin describes in his diary, and a visit of the Duchess of Kent and the Princess Victoria to the Duke of Gloucester on Saturday 14 August, including a royal progress in the rain through the town, an event to which John James alludes in his letter to Miss Corlass of that date; but Cheltenham lacked the geological fascination which Ruskin could find even in the walks of the hotel garden at Matlock, and the town would remain in his memory as one of the 'horrible places' of his life.[49] It is obvious in his diary that he takes more interest in their day's absence from Cheltenham when they visited the Cathedral in Gloucester than in their walks in the city among the gardens and spas crowded with the fashionable. The children may have welcomed the chance to occupy themselves apart from John James who might not have been in the best of humours. At both Matlock and Cheltenham he apparently had found letters awaiting him from George Gray concerned with his role as one of the trustees of the Richardson estate in Perth and his responsibilities for the welfare of his sister's children. The letter at Cheltenham seems to have been particularly nettlesome, provoking John James to write to Gray on 4 August: 'The only benefit I have reaped from the Relationship has been, the having four Children to look after. . . . I know I am committed as a Trustee in Mr. Richardsons affairs but as nothing more.'[50] His efforts to help one of the boys, John Ruskin Richardson, with a wine business in Glasgow appeared thankless at the moment. This nephew, he would write to Gray a year later, was 'a good Lad in some Sorts', but in business he had acted like 'a mere ninny'.[51]

Probably at Cheltenham, then, and certainly before 14 August when John James in his letter to Miss Corlass seems to regard the journal as in hand, the children resume their work on their book, starting now on page 1 with the beginning of the tour. Again we may conjecture that Ruskin made a rough draft to which, according to his later recollection, his father contributed the lively sentence about their first visit to Christ Church cathedral: 'They only let us half in & we soon turned ourselves wholly out for they put us into a seat directly under the organ.'[52] Copying this draft, the children may have been surprised on page 29 to find that they had not reserved enough space, so they skip past the pages devoted to the Cheltenham episode to page 38 where, as already shown, they continue the story. Reaching the bottom of page 44, Ruskin, conceivably dismayed with the larger size of his cousin's handwriting and now obliged to plan a second 'volume' of his diary, finds another five folded sheets of paper of different origin and size, inserts them into each other to form this time a quire of 20 pages, and begins the copying himself. Following his note on page 52 of the place where the Castleton section should have been placed, the children work to complete the story within the space of the second 'volume', John on page 62 resorting to a more compressed hand. Again Mary is relegated to copying the less colourful passages – the relatively dull doings in Cheltenham, for example, while Ruskin copies his transformation of their day in Gloucester cathedral into a climactic conclusion of the diary, in which – as Viljoen observes in a note to me – one can find the germ of his later interpretation of early English Gothic.

From this explanation of the peculiar arrangement of the manuscript Dearden has constructed the Calendar of the Tour, (see pages 23–4), which fits the facts within the diary and related documents.

*   *   *

I have been careful to show as conjecture the idea that Ruskin first composed a rough draft of the diary which the children copied into the two paper books. No such rough draft now exists. Traditionally the diary has been attributed to double authorship. I have already cited John James's comment of 1830 that both of the children had 'kept' the journal; Ruskin's reference of 1885 to the manuscript as 'a piece of joint diary' by Mary Richardson and himself, supplemented by an occasional word by his father; and Collingwood's assignment in 1891 of joint authorship to it. In his citations of the diary in his notes to his edition of Ruskin's poems, Collingwood attributes authorship of each passage according to the handwriting in which it appears. Ruskin's editors follow the same practice in their citations of the diary, although in their Catalogue of Ruskin's diaries, in which the diary of 1830 heads the list, they make no mention of a divided authorship. Viljoen regarded Mary Richardson as Ruskin's collaborator, believing that the children composed the text as they passed the manuscript from one to another. Dearden, not having to confront directly the problem of the authorship of the diary in his edition of Ruskin's *Iteriad*, also regarded it as 'a prose account of the tour kept jointly by John and Mary'.[53] Hunt follows Dearden in describing the diary as a joint production.[54]

Dearden and I now believe, however, that the young Ruskin is the principal composer of the diary. In the descriptions of the works of art which the family saw in the churches and great houses, John James may well have furnished details for his son, and once he literally takes a hand through writing in the manuscript 'by Canova', a name which the young copyists had misspelled. What we have is rightly a 'joint diary', a joint production mostly in the handwriting of the two cousins, but the voice is Ruskin's. Characteristically, as we know from their letters, Ruskin refers to his parents as 'Mamma' and 'Papa', while Mary addresses them as 'Aunt' and 'Uncle'. In three passages in Ruskin's hand in the diary he refers to his parents in his usual way. In only one passage in Mary's hand does she allude to Mrs Ruskin as 'Aunt', and that is on page 2 of the manuscript where in an interlinear passage she contradicts her cousin's description of their second day in Oxford. After their tour of the colleges, Ruskin had written, they 'returned to the inn much pleased'. Using a caret Mary inserts over this line the unpleasant truth: 'trunk carried away, with Aunts watch in it'. In the long passage which Mary copies about their sight-seeing in Liverpool and their travels to the Low Wood Inn on Lake Windermere, she alludes twice to John James as 'Papa' – strong evidence, we think, that she is copying work composed by Ruskin. The unlikely alternatives are to think that this 15-year-old girl is writing from dictation or that she has agreed to make her parts of the diary sound as though they were written by her younger cousin.

The children may have made a game of alternating the task of copying the diary into their two paper books, but it seems improbable that either would stop in mid-sentence to allow the other to compose the remainder of the thought. In none of these mid-sentence breaks is there any change of tone. Indeed the tone is consistent throughout, revealing the style and humour characteristic of Ruskin's letters to his father of this period. In their walk about town on their last day at Oxford they 'danced into the courts of almost all the colleges but always danced out again without seeing anything worthy of being put down', reads a passage in Ruskin's hand. Emerging from the Bradshaw mine, the party was glad to shed the protective garb they had worn, 'our musty fusty dusty rusty coats', so Ruskin writes. In Mary's hand appear phrases that have the ring of her cousin. Observing that the worm had damaged some of the frescoed ceilings at Chatsworth, the writer laments: 'Alas! that such beauty should fall to decay, under the attack of an enemy, so apparently insignificant!!!.' At Windermere the writer decries the bad weather: '. . . alas, the envious tricks of misfortune. . . .' After a busy day at Keswick, Mary writes that the family 'gladly returned in order to pay a visit to Morpheus, who entertained us handsomely all night'. The diary is everywhere reflective of the young Ruskin's interests – art, architecture, mineralogy, and above all his love of landscapes and cloud effects suggestive of the picturesque and sublime, a taste shared by father and son, as Hunt has shown well in his discussion of this diary and the *Iteriad*.[55] The diary also reflects the careful reporting of detail and at times the sense of adventure which the boy had enjoyed the preceding winter in his reading of Bishop Heber's *Narrative of a Journey through . . . India*. 'Tis most delightful', he wrote to his father of this book in March 1829.[56] At no point does the diary suggest either Mary's greater maturity or the feminine interests she would record in 1833 when she kept her own journal of the family's tour of the Continent.[57] About three-quarters of the diary is in Ruskin's hand, a likely reflection of his greater interest in its production.

Whether the diary of 1830 is of single or joint authorship does not detract from its importance as a record of this episode in Ruskin's early life. The diary was soon to prove of value to the boy as he resolved in November of that year to begin *Iteriad*, the little epic in four books about the family's stay in the Lake District on which he worked throughout the following year. The letters from his father, who was travelling again through the Lakes in the early months of 1831, plunged the young poet into a 'pleasing dream' of memories when he wrote to John James: 'I have been with you scaling the heights of Castlerig looking down upon Keswick gazing on the enormous bulk of the mighty Helvellyn or passing by Low-wood happy Low-wood and the sparkling waves of blue Windermere.'[58]Experiences on this tour, as already observed, become transformed into the imagery of his imagination. In 1856, writing of his pleasure in landscape as being his 'ruling passion', Ruskin recalls his crossing of the Shap Fells and being let out of the chaise to run up the hills as among the 'beginnings' of his life.[59] He would not forget the pictures of this past. Visiting Lancaster forty-one years later Ruskin writes to his mother of the inn, probably the King's Arms, where she 'and my father used to come with me, forty years ago. Such ups and downs of stairs and black wood panels and lovely old silk samplers in the bedrooms. . . .'[60]

*　*　*

There being no known portraits of Ruskin between 1822 and 1841, the frontispiece in this volume presents him in his college years, a splendid likeness never before reproduced because it has been in private ownership until Dearden acquired it in 1967 for the Ruskin Galleries. Painted in oil by Thomas Richmond, the elder brother of George Richmond, R. A., perhaps in 1840–41, the picture presents Ruskin in black coat with embroidered waistcoat and floral-patterned stock, holding his gloves, with his hat and cane on a bench behind him. The drawings by Ruskin in this volume are selected to illustrate places the family visits in 1830, although he executed none of them during the tour. It was not until late 1831 that Ruskin, wishing to record the subjects of future travels, took drawing lessons from Charles Runciman to learn the principles of perspective and composition.

Three of these drawings have not been previously published. On their first morning at Oxford, as already noted in the diary, the family went to the chapel of Christ Church to hear the boys sing, and were seated directly under the organ. During his second year at Oxford Ruskin drew the choir facing the organ screen under which he sat on his first visit, the fine pencil drawing in Plate 3 which he presented to Thomas Gaisford, the dean of the college, who had taken an early interest in Ruskin's sketchbooks. In a letter to the dean dated 11 January 1842 Ruskin refers to this drawing of the choir and to a later one of Christ Church[61] which he was also presenting to Gaisford. 'The indulgence with which you formerly received my very poor sketch of the interior of the Cathedral, encourages me to hope for your acceptance of a Drawing of Christ Church', Ruskin begins his letter. The letter and the two drawings remained with descendants of Dean Gaisford and are now in a private collection whose owner has kindly given permission to cite the letter and to reproduce the drawing of the choir.

The second unpublished drawing, Plate 6, is a view of Langdale Pikes from Low Wood Inn on Lake Windermere made in the summer of 1837 when the Ruskins again were visiting the Lakes. It was a scene which the family had admired in 1830 from the same spot, a 'most beautiful view' of the Pikes, '& in the distance, Skawfell rears his giant bulk', so the diary reads. The present location of the original pencil sketch is unknown, but this reproduction comes from a photograph taken for Cook and Wedderburn which is preserved today at Bembridge.

The other drawing published here for the first time, Plate 7, was also made during the summer tour of 1837. In the following year Ruskin included the central part of this drawing of Coniston Hall and the Old Man as an illustration for his chapter on chimneys in his 'Poetry of Architecture' running in Loudon's *Architectural Magazine*.[62] This excised version of the drawing appears to be a view of the Hall and the mountain made from the lake. The foreground detail of the original drawing preserved in the Coniston Museum shows, however, that the sketch was not made from the lake, but from the eastern shore. Dearden assures us that the only point on this shore from which the drawing could have been made is the old harbour at Brantwood. 'Little did Ruskin know when he made this drawing', Dearden writes of this sketch, 'that thirty-four years later he would buy Brantwood, the house directly behind him, and that he would see this scene from his study and bedroom windows daily for the last eleven years of his life. When the Ruskins were at the old Waterhead Inn in 1830, Brantwood on the eastern shore and the Hall on the Western shore of the lake would have been a little over a mile away from them, but probably obscured that day by the weather!' The diary of 1830 makes no mention of Coniston Hall, but on the rainy day in Coniston which the Ruskins were obliged to spend mostly indoors at the Inn at the head of the lake they did see the misty outlines of the Old Man.

The approach to Warwick Castle, Ruskin writes in the diary of 1830, 'was very beautiful between rocks overgrown with ivy' – the view which he drew in 1847 from the bridge crossing the Avon in which Guy's Tower and Caesar's Tower may be seen emerging from the trees (Plate 4). The street scene in Derby drawn on Ruskin's tour to the Lakes in 1837 (Plate 5), which Dearden has described elsewhere as one of the fine drawings of the period, shows a tall house in the foreground with 'a gable end which obviously interested Ruskin', and on the opposite side of the street a small medieval public house, some Georgian buildings, and finally the tower of All Saints, now Derby Cathedral.[63]

Ruskin would sketch interior scenes of Haddon Hall on both his tours of the Lakes in 1837 and 1838, but he records in the second drawing (Plate 8) the great dining hall mentioned in the diary of 1830. Visiting Gloucester Cathedral in 1830 Ruskin describes in the diary the beauty and strength of the tower, '& yet it is so light, so airy & seemingly so frail that it appears as if the 1st tempest . . . would hurl it into destruction', qualities he would record in his drawing of the tower probably in the summer of 1834 (Plate 9). It was 'a really pretty drawing', he wrote of it later. 'I had constructed a style of pen-drawing with shade stippled out of doubled lines, and outline carefully broken for picturesqueness, yet not inelegant. . . .'[64]

* * *

Note on the text

Dearden takes the text of the diary from the holograph in the Morgan Library (MA3451), but he presents it in the sequence in which the tour actually took place, as I explained above in my discussion of the Calendar of the Tour. That is, Dearden transcribes the pages of the manuscript in this order: pages 1–28; 38–52; 29–38; 52–64.

In his transcript of the text he preserves the original punctuation and spelling. Although about one-quarter of the diary is in Mary Richardson's hand, the punctuation of the entire manuscript is characteristic of Ruskin's practice as we find it in his letters of this period. Still tutored at home, the boy usually capitalizes the beginning of his sentences and closes them with appropriate punctuation, but he will also run sentences together or separate them only with a comma. To aid the reader, Dearden has separated run-on sentences by extra space. Because of John James's insistence on economy in the use of paper, his family in their letters ordinarily did not indent paragraphs but usually left a wider space or a long dash between sentences to indicate a shift in the thought. For purposes of greater clarity, Dearden has introduced paragraphing in the text where these signals or sometimes the sense suggest it. Where a paragraph would begin with a lower case letter, Dearden substitutes a capital letter enclosed in square brackets. Significant words which the copyist wrote and crossed out are set within shallow brackets like this: < . . . > Those sections of the manuscript in Mary Richardson's hand appear in italics. Again, to improve the clarity of the diary, Dearden has introduced the approximate date at the beginning of each daily entry.

Unless otherwise indicated, citations from manuscripts in the notes are hitherto unpublished.

Van Akin Burd
Companion of the Guild of St George
Cortland, New York

Notes

1 Letter to James S. Dearden, dated 4 Nov. 1968 (carbon ts., Van A. Burd).

2 James S. Dearden, 'John Ruskin: Lakeland Tourist,' *Cumbria* ns 10 (1960): 163–7. Rpt. in Dearden, *Facets of Ruskin* 46–54.

3 *The Works of John Ruskin*, 39 vols. (London: Allen, 1903–12), hereafter referred to as *Works*, XXXV: 622.

4 *The Poems of John Ruskin*, 2 vols. (Orpington: Allen, 1891) I: 266.

5 *Works* II: 534.

6 MS. Eng. misc. c. 234, fols. 2–27. The transcript was deposited in the Library in 1936.

7 *The Diaries of John Ruskin*, 3 vols. (Oxford: 1956–9). The editors were unaware of the transcript of the 1830 diary in the Bodleian Library.

8 *Works* XXXVIII: 204.

9 W. G. Collingwood, *The Life of John Ruskin*, 6th ed. (London: Methuen, 1905) 30–32.

10   More recently, as already noted, J. S. Dearden included in the notes to his edition of *Iteriad* two of the passages from the diary cited by the previous editors and a few more excerpts; through H. G. Viljoen's courtesy, I cited the diary in my edition of *The Ruskin Family Letters*, 2 vols. (Ithaca: Cornell UP, 1973), hereafter referred to in these notes as *RFL*, I: 249n4. In 1976 Robert Hewison, using the transcript of the diary in the Bodleian Library, cited two passages from Ruskin's description of the pictures which the family saw on the tour (*John Ruskin: The Argument of the Eye* [Princeton UP, 1976] 15). John Dixon Hunt seems to be the only one of the recent biographers of Ruskin who has examined the manuscript diary since its arrival at the Morgan Library, and he quotes two previously uncited passages (*The Wider Sea: A Life of John Ruskin* [London: Dent, 1982] 33, 45).

11   *Works* XXXIV: 571.

12   *Works* XXXV: 29–32. The chariot in Plate 2 formerly belonged to the Baskerville family and is now preserved at the Industrial Museum, Wollaton Hall, Nottingham.

13   Letter of 23–4 Feb. 1822, *RFL* I: 117–18.

14   *Works* XXXV: 105.

15   *Works* XXXVIII: 339.

16   *Works* V: 365. After Ruskin's death a memorial monolith of Borrowdale stone bearing a bronze portrait medallion by Andrea C. Lucchesi and part of this quotation, was unveiled on Friar's Crag on 6 Oct. 1900. Its site became the National Trust's first Lake District property.

    For Ruskin's visit to Coniston in 1824, see Collingwood, *Poems* I: 276nxxi. For his stay at Keswick the same year, see Collingwood, *Life* 17.

17   *RFL* I: 137.

18   Margaret Ruskin in letter to John James Ruskin, 7–8 May 1826, *RFL* I: 139.

19   'On Scotland', *Works* II: 256.

20   'On Skiddaw and Derwent Water', *Works* II: 265–6. Although Cook dates the poem 1828 (*Works* II: 265), Ruskin's letter to his father of 10 May 1829 suggests that he had been composing it earlier that year (*RFL* I: 199). The poem became Ruskin's first published work: *Spiritual Times*, 10 (1830): 72–3. For the inclusion of Coniston on the family visit of 1826, see Collingwood, *Poems* I: 276nxxi.

21   His letter to Margaret Ruskin, 23 Feb. 1827, *RFL* I: 152.

22 *Life* 30.

23 *Praeterita, Works* XXXV: 71.

24 Letter from Plymouth dated 25 May 1828 (ALS, MS. Eng. Lett. d. 227, Bodley).

25 Shakespeare's Birthplace Visitors' Book (DR 185/4, p. 351), Birthplace Trust, Stratford-on-Avon.

26 *Praeterita, Works* XXXV: 71, 131.

27 Letter from Ruskin to his father, 15 Jan. 1833, *RFL* I: 274.

28 John James Ruskin's annual account book and his Summary account book (MS 28, MS 30, Ruskin Galleries, Bembridge) show that in 1829 he bought the lease of 28 Herne Hill for £2200. In 1830 he paid the Camberwell bricklayer William Barnes a total of £124 10s. for pointing the house. He also paid the house furnishers William and Edward Snell of Albemarle Street, the sum of £1675 for 'additions to house', and a further £545 13s 9d for other items. The work continued in 1831 for the accounts of this year show payments to Snell for painting, furniture, carpets, and other furnishings, mainly for John's and Mary's rooms.

29 *RFL* I: 218n2.

30 Letter dated 30 Nov. 1829, *RFL* I: 209–10n4.

31 Letter from Margaret Ruskin to J. J. Ruskin, 20 Oct. 1829, *RFL* I: 203.

32 ALS, MS. Eng. Lett. d. 227, Bodley.

33 Letter dated Monday, 'Cheltenham 16 Aug. 1830'. Because John James refers in his letter to events of the preceding Saturday, he probably intended to date it 14 August (Ryl. Eng. MS. 1304/1, The John Rylands University Library of Manchester).

34 Her letter dated 20 Oct. 1829, *RFL* I: 203.

35 His letter dated 26 Oct. 1829, *RFL* I: 205.

36 MS 28, Ruskin Galleries, Bembridge.

37 *Works* XXXV: 32–3.

38 *Iteriad*: 27.

39 See note 33 above.

40 See note 25 above and Chatsworth Visitors' Book, Devonshire collections, Chatsworth, Bakewell, Derbyshire.

41 George May, *The History of Evesham* (Evesham: 1834) 216.

42 ALSs, MS. Eng. Lett. d. 227, Bodley.

43 For the DePree family see *RFL* I: 19n3. A volume first used by John James and then as a diary by his son contains at pp. 1–21 John James's list of the family tours. On page 1 is the entry: '1830 Tour May 18, Oxford Leam[ingto]n, Matlock, Chatsworth, Dove-

dale, Keswick, Buttermere, Coniston, Castleton, Bakewell, Birm-[ingha]m, Glouc[ceste]r, Oxford, Langley.' (MS 18, Bembridge)

44   ALS, MS. Eng. Lett. d. 227, Bodley. Collingwood writes, perhaps in error, that the Ruskins returned to Herne Hill in September (*Poems* I: 258).

45   Because the pages at this time had not been numbered, Ruskin was unable to fill in the figure, leaving a blank space.

46   Dearden, *Facets* 73.

47   The subscription book of the Pump Room of the Pittville Spa in Cheltenham lists the Ruskins as subscribers for walks in Pittville Park but not for use of the waters. They could have taken waters elsewhere in the town.

48   *Works* XXXV: 75.

49   *Works* XXXV: 75; XXXVIII: 338.

50   ALS, MS. Eng. Lett. d. 227, Bodley.

51   Letter dated 6 Sept. 1831, cited in *RFL* I: 277n5.

52   Dearden informs me that F. J. Sharp, observing that in the manuscript of the diary this sentence is clearly in Ruskin's hand, wrote in the margin of his set of the *Works* (XXXV: 622): 'Ruskin is in error here; this part is in Ruskin's writing, and in trusting to memory made a mistake.' Dearden points out, however, that Ruskin may have been recalling the rough draft of the diary to which John James contributed this sentence.

53   *Iteriad* 18.

54   *The Wider Sea* 44.

55   *The Wider Sea* 41–2.

56   *RFL* I: 193.

57   MS HM 41910–41913, The Huntington Library.

58   Letter dated 14 Mar. 1851, *RFL* I: 249.

59   *Works* V: 365.

60   Letter dated 11 Sept. 1871 (ALS, B VI, Bembridge).

61   The drawing of Christ Church is reproduced in *Works* XXXV: Pl. IX.

62   *Works* I: 60, Fig. 10.

63   This drawing of Derby was first reproduced in James S. Dearden's essay, 'John Ruskin's Tour to the Lake District in 1837', *Connoisseur* 167 (Mar. 1968): 165–8. Rpt. without the drawing in Dearden, *Facets* 55–62, from which I take the citation on p. 60.

64   *Works* XXXV: 621–2. Ruskin probably errs in recalling 1832 as the date of the drawing. Cook and Wedderburn date it as 'probably 1834' (*Works* XXI: 193n).

Calendar of the tour

Tues	18 May	Herne Hill, Ealing, Uphall, Uxbridge, Gerrards Cross, *Oxford*
Wed–Fri	19–21	*Oxford*
Sat	22	Oxford, Blenheim, *Woodstock*
Sun	23	*Woodstock*
Mon	24	Woodstock, *Worcester*
Tues	25	Worcester, Stratford, Warwick, *Leamington*
Wed–Fri	26–28	*Leamington*
Sat	29	*Leamington*, Warwick Castle
Sun	30	*Leamington*
Mon	31	Leamington, *Birmingham*
Tues	1 June	*Birmingham*
Wed	2	Birmingham, *Lichfield*
Thurs	3	*Lichfield*
Fri	4	Lichfield, Derby, Kedleston, *Matlock*
Sat–Mon	5–7	*Matlock*
Tues	8	Matlock, Dovedale, *Thorpe*
Wed	9	
Thurs	10	
Fri	11	Haddon Hall, Chatsworth
Sat–Sun	12–13	*Buxton*
Mon	14	Buxton, *Manchester*
Tues	15	Manchester, *Liverpool*
Wed	16	*Liverpool* (railway)
Thurs	17	Liverpool (cemetery)
Fri	18	Liverpool, *Preston*
Sat–Sun	19–20	*Preston*
Mon	21	Preston, Garstang, Lancaster, *Kendal*
Tues	22	Kendal, *Low Wood*, walk to Ambleside
Wed	23	Low Wood, Grasmere, *Keswick*
Thurs	24	*Keswick*, Friar's Crag

Fri	25	*Keswick*, Crosthwaite's museum
Sat	26	*Keswick*
Sun	27	*Keswick*, Crosthwaite Church
Mon	28	*Keswick*, Lodore, Borrowdale, Bowder Stone, Honister
Tues	29	*Keswick*
Wed	30	*Keswick*, Skiddaw
Thurs	1 July	Keswick, Penrith, Troutbeck, Ullswater, *Patterdale*
Fri	2	Patterdale, *Low Wood*
Sat	3	*Low Wood* (fishing)
Sun	4	*Low Wood*, Rydal Chapel
Mon	5	*Low Wood* (on lake)
Tues	6	*Low Wood*, Coniston
Wed–Fri	7–9	*Low Wood*
Sat	10	Low Wood, *Bowness*
Sun	11	*Bowness*
Mon	12	Bowness, *Kendal*
Tues	13	Kendal, Kirkby Lonsdale, Lancaster, Garstang, *Preston*
Wed	14	Preston, Chorley, Bolton, *Manchester*
Thurs	15	Manchester, Stockport, Disley, Chapel-en-le-Frith, *Castleton*
Fri	16	*Castleton*, Peak Cavern, Speedwell Mine, Mam Tor, Winnats
Sat	17	*Castleton*, Sheffield
Sun	18	*Castleton*, Hope Church, Peverill Castle
Mon	19	Castleton, Bradshaw Mine, *Matlock*
Tues	20–	*Matlock*
Sun	1 Aug	
Mon	2	Matlock, Ashbourne, Uttoxeter, Stafford, Penkridge, Wolverhampton, Stourbridge, *Bromsgrove*
Tues	3	Bromsgrove, Tewkesbury, Gloucester, *Cheltenham*
Wed–Mon	4–16	*Cheltenham*
Tues	17	Cheltenham, returning via Oxford and Langley, perhaps spending a night at each
About Thurs	19	London

Note: The town where the Ruskins spent each night appears in italics.

Figure 1 Map of England showing the routes taken on the 1830 tour

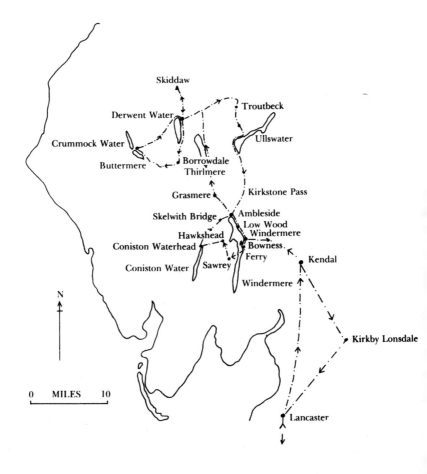

Figure 2 Map of the Lake District showing the routes taken

A tour to the Lakes in Cumberland

18 May 1830, Tuesday, London   We set off from London at 7 oclock on Tuesday Morning 18 May and passing through Ealing[1] we proceeded towards Uphall[2] where we intended to have breakfasted but the house looking rather queer we only changed horses & went on through Uxbridge to Geralds cross where we breakfasted

The room was fitted up with some taste (although plainly)   we had an excellent breakfast but what was still better in the adjoining room was a library with a good many volumes in it by the best authors   The room looked out on the entrance to the Duke of Portlands grounds which are open to the inn & altogether the place was very pleasant.[3]

Leaving Geralds cross we proceeded towards Oxford.[4] The day was extremely hot & the sky was extremely blue but it was rather windy & of course rather dusty. Coming to a long & steep hill we all got out except Mamma & walked up   We arrived at Oxford about 4 oclock to dinner. After we had dined we went out & came to Christchurch college[5]   We entered a spacious gateway which opened to a large square court surrounded by a terrace about 3 feet high above which rose the college in fine old Gothic turrets & in the middle of the court was a small pond   We then returned home.

19 May, Wednesday, Oxford   The following morning we went to Christchurch chapel to hear the boys sing. They only let us half in & we soon turned ourselves wholly out for they put us in a seat directly under the organ.

We then went to the New college[6] and first entered the chapel   we went up to the altar piece & looked at five beautiful pieces of sculpture the 1st representing the <ascension> annunciation the 2nd the nativity 3rd the descent from the cross 4th the resurrection & 5th the ascension   We next saw the bishops crosier   it was silver gilt inlaid with precious stones & with several pictures done in enamel. The windows each consisted of a picture of some saint or Martyr of the Romish Church   At the west <side> end of the church was a large window representing the nativity & below were the three christian virtues faith hope & charity & the 4 cardinal patience fortitude justice & prudence

We next went to the amphitheatre[7] an immense room which would hold three thousand 500 persons comfortably   it was built after the amphitheatre at Rome. Opposite the vice chancellors chair were 3 portraits   in the centre was his Majesty George the 4th & on <each> one side a picture of the emperor of Russia & on the other the king of Prussia

We next came to the Ratcliffe library[8]which like most other libraries had books in it. We saw cases containing specimens of Alabaster marble &cc   There were also several fine statues & busts. We then went up to the top on the outside & had a beautiful view of all Oxford with the colleges ∧ ∧ *trunk carried away, with Aunts watch in it* we then returned to the inn much pleased

20 May, Thursday, Oxford   The next day we went to see Magdalene College[9] There was a most curious stone pulpit projecting from the wall   it looked out upon the court *We then passed through several inner courts, & saw Addison's room's, small tho' prettily fitted up, we then went into the Chapel and saw a beautiful Window representing the day of Judgement, in the centre in the clouds was Christ seated on his throne   on one side were the blessed ascending to heaven, at his feet were the twelve Apostles, on the other side at the bottom was Satan dragging, the wicked into hell, and grinning horribly a Ghastly smile. Lightning was seen striking them down. Magdalene College library was a very pleasant room, with a good many books in it, at one end was a most beautiful picture of our Saviour bearing his cross   it was long supposed to have been painted by* Guido but [was] lately ascertained to have been done by Morelles.

Leaving Magdalène College we went to Christchurch & saw the large hall where the students dined.[10] There were ninetynine pictures amongst which were those of Henry the 8th Cardinal Wolsey Mr Canning & Doctor Busby of flogging memory &c

That afternoon we went to the waterside to see the students rowing in jumping out of a boat   one nearly fell into the water but he escaped.

21 May, Friday, Oxford   The next day we took a walk in the town & danced into the courts of almost all the colleges but always danced out again without seeing anything worthy of being put down. In the evening we saw some Morrice dancers.

22 May, Saturday, Oxford   The next day we left Oxford & got to Blenheim to breakfast   We then went to see the duke of Marlboroughs house.[11] There were a great many invaluable pictures by Rubens Guido Carlo Dulce Teniers Rembrandt Sir Joshua Reynolds & Many others   There was one picture of Charles the 1st on horseback which was pronounced by Sir Joshua Reynolds to be *the finest equestrian piece he had ever seen. There was also a most beautiful picture by Carlo Dolce & a very fine Bacchanalian piece by Rubens. There was a very pleasing picture of the late Duke & Duchess & their six eldest Children by Sir Joshua Reynolds*   We then entered the library where was a beautiful statue of Queen Anne by Rysbrack, the sculpture of which cost 5,000 pounds. It was the most beautiful library <I> we ever saw.

We then had a delightful walk in the park. & saw the remains of a fine old oak which had been struck & set fire to by lightning and had not the engines been brought to play upon it would have set fire to the trees around it   *some of the oak trees the gardener said were upwards of 700 years old*   We then went to a beautiful pheasantry. there were several Beautiful gold & silver pheasant & a peacock who erected his tail & strutted with all the pride of a duke himself.   we then returned home.

23 May, Sunday, Woodstock   The next day (Sunday) we went to church[12] it was a nice old place though not fine   The same afternoon there was a tremendous thunderstorm.   the lightning was extremely vivid.

24 May, Monday, Woodstock   We set off from Woodstock on Monday morning for Worcester   we had a pleasant <ride>

<road> ride but it was very wet[13] In the afternoon we went to see
Worcester Cathedral   There were several fine monuments one
especially to Bishop Hough by Roubilliac   We next saw the tomb of
King John   the sexton told us that his body really lay there that the
tomb had been opened about 30 years ago when the body was found in
good preservation. We saw also the tomb of prince Arthur   there
was a great deal of very fine sculpture about it although much
dilapidated   we saw nothing more of any importance.

25 May, Tuesday, Worcester

We left Worcester next morning
at 7 oclock & got to Stratford upon Avon[14] to breakfast   we visited
Shakespeares tomb a bust of him was in a niche between two small
black Corinthian pillars   we next went to the room Where he was
born   it was a very old place & the walls all scratched over with
names among which were several of the royal family but a great many
were effaced   Sir Walter Scott had been there twice. *There was a box
made of the wood of a Mulberry tree, which Shakespeare had planted*

We then set off for Leamington[15]   We passed through Warwick
in our way.

26 May, Wednesday – 31 May, Monday, Leamington

Leamington is a pleasant place but it was so wet all the time we were
there that we could hardly get out.

On Saturday we went to see Warwick Castle.[16] the approach was
very beautiful between rocks overgrown with ivy. As you enter the
castle the tower over the gateway is called the dock tower that on the
right Guys tower & that on the left Caesars tower   We first entered
the armoury. There was a complete suit belonging to the Warwick
family[17]   above it was the helmet of Oliver Cromwell also a <suit>
coat of Buff in which Lord [Brooke] was killed   We then passed
through a range of apartments which looked out upon the river. there
were a great many fine pictures but the house being undergoing
repairs they were out of their places & in such bad lights that we could
not see them   there were several by Salvator Rosa[18] & Vandyke[19] a
pair of fine lions by Rubens &c.[20] The ceilings were extremely fine.

Leaving the castle we took a walk in the grounds which were very
beautiful. In the greenhouse was a

Punch bowl

beautiful vase[21] which was sent to King George the 3rd from a village
near Rome   It is so well known we need not give a description of it.
As we returned home we had a beautiful view of the castle from the

bridge   we had a very pleasant walk to Leamington. [The word Punch Bowl is written in large letters across this section of the manuscript.]

We went to the church on Sunday & had a very comfortable seat. there was nothing uncommon to be seen

On Monday we left Leamington & went on to Birmingham which was almost worse than London itself   such smoky dirty narrow streets that two carriages could hardly pass & such a hill in one part of the town We got a most delightful room & very good bedrooms.[22] the afternoon was very wet but

1 June, Tuesday, Birmingham   the next day being a little better we got out and went first to a small museum in which was a very nice collection of British birds & insects.[23] We then went to a pin manufactory & were much pleased with seeing the number of processes the wire has to go through before it becomes the bright smooth pointed pin.[24] That evening <we> Papa & I went to the theatre[25] but it was so badly acted that we soon came away

2 June, Wednesday, Birmingham   We were glad to get out of Birmingham the next morning and to breathe the fresh air again   the day was extremely fine & we had a delightful ride to Lichfield.

3 June, Thursday, Lichfield   The next morning we went to see the cathedral   there was a beautiful monument of two sisters by Chantry   they both lost their lives by accident the eldest bursting a bloodvessel by too much exertion and the youngest burnt to death while her governess left her for a few moments   the youngest held a bunch of snowdrops one could have fancied them lying asleep with their arms around one anothers necks[26]   there were also some most beautiful painted windows which were almost invaluable but a gentleman in the time of the Revolution procured them for two hundred pounds[27]   there were several other monuments particularly one to Lady M. W. Montague[28] there were some lines underneath another[29] by Sir Walter Scott We also saw the chapter house a very nice comfortable room warmed by a stove. Returning home we saw the house[30] where Dr Johnson was born.

4 June, Friday, Lichfield   Leaving Lichfield we went on to Derby which is a large town but we could get no pleasant walks about it   We went to see a silk manufactory[31] but it was a holiday & hardly any of the workmen were there

5 June, Saturday, Derby   [T]he next day we went to see the estate of Lord Scarsdale.[32] it had a most beautiful approach over a bridge. Coming into the Corinthian hall as it was called we looked at 24 massive fluted pillars of solid alabaster which were of the Corinthian order. there were numbers of busts & statues amongst which was one of Apollo   the next room was extremely light and elegant although not large. there were numbers of beautiful pictures by the finest old masters. the pillars of the drawing room are of fine variegated alabaster   *there were several painted imitations of carved ivory, which at a little distance we really mistook for it,*

    [T]he road from Derby to Matlock is very beautiful but owing to a heavy shower of rain, which came on just as we came out of Lord Scarsdale's, & continued all the rest of the day, we could hardly see anything.

    Matlock Bath is a most delightful place[33]   the river Derwent winds at the foot of some beautiful rocks which are partly <covered> hidden with trees & the bank of the river next to the inn is also covered with them. We got a beautiful room with a fine bow window

6 June, Sunday – 8 June, Tuesday, Matlock   The next day we took a delightful walk by the side of the Derwent   it was extremely high with the late rain & I have seldom seen the sea rise into such waves as rolled along the base of the high Tor[34] which is an extremely high rock standing like a gigantic tower above the river Derwent   Returning home we tried a mountain path which came along the side of the hill   we got on very well for some time but presently we had nearly stuck in the mire and had some difficulty in getting across a puddle which extended over the path   the rest of the path was extremely dirty & we soon came to a complete stop & were forced to return   our shoes were wet through & we were glad to get home again.

    [A]t Matlock we had some fine rambling scrambling walks one especially. We got up to the top of a hill & wishing to get down again a different way than that by which we came up we scrambled over a stone wall & after all our trouble fell into a disagreeable stony <path> road that we had been in no less than 3 times. However we still found another path & danced down the hill very merrily but were much astonished to find ourselves stopped by a gate and a woman who said we must not go through without paying 6d each   We had nothing for it but to retrace our steps & were forced after all to return home by the old stony path.

We also went to see the Grand Devonshire cavern[35] lately discovered   we had each a candle & some other preparations for a few drops of water as our guide said that we must be a little wetted   we entered the place & passed for a few hundred yards through an old lead mine   then coming into the cavern we passed between rocks of calcareous spar with here & there a pretty heavy shower   there were several very awkward steps to ascend & at some places a pretty deep & wide hole but these were all fenced off so that there was not much danger of falling into them. *At one part there was a beautiful Bengal light which illumed the sides & roof of the cavern very beautifully, showing of what they were composed. we came out of this cavern, at a much higher part, of the mountain, than where we <went in> entered. We then went down to the river side, & in passing thro' the museum garden, we saw a beautiful hawk, we then crossed the river Derwent, & ascended the cliffs on the opposite side we had a very pleasant walk & a delightful view*

We also saw Sir Richard Arkwrights grounds[36] which were very beautiful but nothing very particular   from one point you have a delightful opening between two hills   on your right are some fine rocks & before you rolls the river Derwent   There was a fine pinery & several beautiful graperys   the house looked very handsome but we only saw the outside   we also had a fine view from the cliffs facing our own inn.

[W]e had many fine walks &c & we bought as good many minerals vases &c amongst which was a beautiful Adrian vase of Italian alabaster also a Roman <sarcophagus costing 50 shillings> bath in black marble elastic bitumen &c[37]

8 June, Tuesday, Matlock

On Tuesday we set off from Matlock on our way to Dovedale & arrived at the Dog & Partridge[38] but were somewhat astounded on being ushered into a room of no very promising appearance with a brick floor without a carpet & extremely small   However we got a carpet laid down & the articles being very good we enjoyed our breakfast quite as much & perhaps more than we did at any of the great fashionable hotels

After breakfast having procured a guide we walked to Dove dale about a mile distant from the inn   you enter the dale[39] by the side of Thorpe Cloud one of the highest mountains of the dale of a very singular conical shape   Turning round the side of Thorpe Cloud you have the first view of the river Dove which rolls itself beautifully at the foot of the hills   Proceeding onwards the first objects of any importance are the Sugarloaves[40] as immense conical fragments of rock on your left hand are called   you next see Dovedale castle a very beautiful mass *of rock, next comes Dovedale Church, which was also very fine, opposite the latter on your right hand, are the 12 Apostles, large pieces of rocks a little farther on, on the same side is Reynard's cave, consisting of a wonderful natural arch, of rock standing by itself, beyond which is the main entrance to the Cavern, but we did not go so far as this, the path to it is extremely steep, & the stones being all loose gave way under our feet, we then returned by the same path we had previously pursued, which was very dirty indeed.* And in some cases we could hardly get across. We enjoyed our walk very much & got home to dinner.

11 June, Friday, Thorpe   On Friday morning at 7 oclock we set off for Haddon hall[41] part of this extremely old baronial residence was built before the time of William the Conqueror   We had a beautiful view of it from the road   Having come to the entrance we had to stoop our heads to get under a very low door which conducts you into the inner court   a hole about a foot and a half deep is worn in the stone by the pressure of the foot

We first came into the chaplains sitting room which was very ghostly   there was an old cavalry boot which had a heel about two inches high & a sole proportionably thick   There was also a pair of pistol cases of rather an uncouth shape and beside them lay an old gun which was very rusty & had a very odd shaped butt   in a small adjoining closet there were two padlocks which had fastened the gates of the castle about six inches long and the dishes which were served up to table of which the largest was about two feet long & the smallest about a foot <& a half> these were soup plates which at moderate computation were above 8 inches deep

We then saw the great dining hall   there were originally three large tables but only one remained. The chapel had once some very beautiful painted windows but the greatest part of them had been stolen away one night & only a few fragments remained to show us what they had once been   at the door was a very narrow [?] stair which had once been intended to wind up the clock of which the remains were shown us as we then went into the drawing room a very old place   there was a bow window in a recess which we supposed had once been thought a very pleasant corner but there were so many thick pillars dividing it that in the present age it would be considered very disagreeable we saw also several old chairs which seemed to have been very easy but were so crazy it was not safe to sit down in them.

[W]e passed through several sitting rooms in which we saw nothing particular except rotten tapestry. we then went into the ballroom & picture gallery   there was one picture in it very well painted but very old   it was very long & there was some old carved woodwork which had once been very beautiful.

There was also a bust of an aunt of the Duke of Rutland's, taken after death & looked extremely ghastly, as she would not have her likeness taken while alive   from thence we proceeded to a bed chamber in which was a very old bed which was very rich   the satin was as soft as the present but it was so thick that it felt like leather   it was figured with gold wire & was extremely rich.

[W]e then went a little higher & passed through a great many little rooms in which there was nothing particular and thence returning by the great dining hall we went into the kitchen where a fireplace was shown us where they roasted a whole ox & 12 sheep every day. we then went through several other rooms belonging to the kitchen such as the scullery   the place where they hung up the quarters for use   the pantry &c

[W]e thence proceeded to the garden which was very full of moss & the trees were very ancient   passing through the garden we re-entered the house & passing through the inner court we bade farewell to this extremely old castle.

[T]he day was very fine & we trotted on much pleased to Chatsworth[42] After breakfast we walked through the park in order to see the *Duke of Devonshire's* house which was repairing   we passed through a fine gateway of a very singular kind of sandstone resembling marble   as we passed by a sort of court we saw through a window a most beautiful gilt vase with a smaller one[43]

[W]e first entered a fine hall with beautiful pillars from which we ascended by a fine staircase with pilasters of Devonshire marble into the entrance hall   in the centre was a beautiful statue of Mars & Cupid and the sides were adorned with numerous busts amongst which were several antiques brought <(from Herculaneum)> at the opposite end to that at which we entered <we ascended> there were two fine staircases one on each side which met at the top   from this point you have a fine view of the hall. *There was a very fine bust of Alexander and several other distinguished individuals. from thence we went to the Chapel, the sides of which were beautifully ornamented with finely carved wood, there was nothing more particularly worthy of attention.*

There was a very long gallery filled with numberless sketches, by the best

masters amongst which were some by Carlo Dolce, Claude Lorraine, Rembrandt, Caracci, Urbini &c they were wonderfully done, and every touch shewed the hand of a master, some appeared to be so carelessly thrown off, you could hardly distinguish the outline, but yet such an effect was produced you could easily see, whose hand pencil had touched the canvas,

[W]e passed thro' several many other rooms; several of the fireplaces, were surrounded with Birds, fruit, flowers &c of carved wood & the corners of the ceilings were ornamented in the same manner, but we were sorry to observe, that the worm had got in to several of the finest parts. Alas! that such beauty should fall to decay. under the attack of an enemy, so apparently insignificant!!!

[I]n one of the apartments, were two large, Indian Chests, beautifully inlaid with brass gold & silver & steel. there was also a large case filled with remains of antiques executed in different kinds of Marble. In the picture gallery were 2 beautiful vases of red Porphyry from Sweden. In the Duke's private apartments, we saw a beautiful statue of Hebe, by Canova, on each side there was a marble table, each supported by 4 vulture's beautifully carved, there were 3 busts on each table, one of which was particularly fine. in another apartment was a statue of Endymion, with a fine hound, reclining by his side & gazing on him with apparent delight, on one side of Endymion was a very handsome sarcophagus, of fine Marble, on the other was a fine Ganymede, one of his arms was thrown round the neck of the bird of <u>love</u> which stood beside him, with expanded wings & seemed impatient for flight, in another part of the room was a table of the finest Malachite   throughout the apartments were a great many tables, vases, &c of the various kinds of Derbyshire marble. Amongst the various busts, there was a very fine one of Buonaparte by Canova. There was also a very fine <picture> statue of Buonapartes mother in a sitting position by Canova. In coming out we saw a full length figure of Mary Queen of Scotts by Westmacot.

We then went into the grounds[44] which are beautiful to see the waterworks. There is a steep hill from the house at the top of which there is a sort of temple erected before which is a small pond in which are two beautiful fountains. there are various figures about the roof & sides of the temple such as lions heads frogs dolphins griffins &c from the mouths of which water spouts   the floor of the temple is full of small holes & when the visitors are enticed into it the water spouts up from these holes & wets them to the skin. The water overflows the rim of the bason which receives it & tumbles down a flight of sides [? sized] steps to the bottom of the hill where it is received in a sort of trough shaped pool; the bottom of which is covered with large stones amongst which the water disappears.

In another part of the grounds is a copper tree from the leaves &

twigs of which the water plays but this was worn out & at the time we were there was repairing. Near this is another wetting decoy. The visitors are enticed to feel the warmth of the water in a small basin. and when they are once feeling there are small pipes concealed in the turf which spout up all round them.

[I]n another part there is a large sheet of water in the centre of which is a jet upwards of 90 feet high and before the house is another smaller fountain consisting of a figure of trion on his dolphin   in the centre are four seahorses around him from all of which there is a jet

[A]fter viewing these works we returned to the inn & set off for Buxton. When you arrive within a few miles of that town the country begins to appear very wild & you pass through several glens formed by bare hills.[45]

Buxton lies in a hollow surrounded by hills   the principal part and indeed almost the only part is the crescent consisting of three large hotels[46] it is faced by a small hill upon which are gravel walks

12 June, Saturday, Buxton   The first evening there was a band of music but we were disappointed the next night for it did not play

13 June, Sunday, Buxton   On Sunday we went to the Church   the minister was very young but he gave us a very good sermon   we were surprised to hear on returning to the inn that he had a wife & family   we then took a very pleasant walk in a large garden near the inn   the walks were very long & being walled in by trees you never could find out where they would end. Buxton is very dull   you could hardly see a single person out of doors.

14 June, Monday, Buxton   On Monday we left[47] Buxton for Manchester in a tremendous shower of rain   the road wound round the hills amongst which Buxton is situated & every now & then as we turned their sharp points a blast came which had great skill in playing on the flute. however we soon got out of this most bleak region & after going a few miles the country became the same as usual

Manchester[48] is a most disagreeable town & we thought it the more so as we had hardly an hour of fair weather all the time we were there   it is so full of manufactorys that you are enveloped in clouds of smoke & the place is so hot we could scarcely breath & were very glad to breathe the fresh air of the country again the next morning.

15 June, Tuesday, Manchester   But when we were already to
set off we found we had got a wrong cloak & to our great chagrin we
found that some person had run away with ours & left their own. The
owner of the cloak could not be discovered & we were forced to take the
cloak promising to send it back when our own should be found

[W]e then gladly set off for Liverpool[49] it soon began to rain &
hardly afterwards ceased so that we did not enjoy our ride so much as
we otherwise would have done but coming out of the smoky atmosphere of Manchester everything was refreshing to us.

We arrived at Liverpool to dinner[50]   it is a very large town
situated on the Mersey a noble river and indeed at Liverpool it is more
an arm of the sea being about a mile and a half across. we were at a
good distance from the waterside   nevertheless we made frequent
excursions to it. The day after we arrived we made an expedition which
I put into rhyme.

> One morning we heard that a ship[51] for New York
> at eve was to sail from the city
> Thought we if we miss seeing her out of port
> it will be a terrible pity.
>
> So at 5 we set off & we came to the shore
> But the ship for to sail was not ready
> And so we did saunter a little time more
> Till our legs they became rather heavy
>
> But our time it wore out & we knew we must go
> & so for that job were preparing
> But still we could not avoid saying no no
> & so we remained there staring
>
> But the ship was so long & our time was quite done
> And so we returned with sorrow
> We mournfully thought as we walked towards home
> That the tide would be later tomorrow
>
> But surprise and dismay did our progress await
> For when we did come to the lock
> We found with surprise they had opened the gate
> & that we were quite come to a stop
>
> But we knew twas in vain this mishap to bewail
> & so our steps we did retrace
> We thought that the other gate might not so fail
> & wished we were out of this place
>
> To our joy we did find that the gate was just closing
> & so we ran onto the lock
> But there was a sailor our progress opposing
> & we were obliged for to stop

But when it was closed & then what a rush
to get over to one side or tother
Our cheeks with the hurry were all in a flush
we had such a terrible pother

16 June, Wednesday, Liverpool   *On Wednesday we went to call on a friend, and in returning, we went to see the Manchester & Liverpool railroad,*[52] *it proceeds underground for the space of two miles. Goods may be conveyed on it from Liverpool to Manchester a distance of 31 miles, and back again, in the space of 3 hours.*

17 June, Thursday, Liverpool   *The following day we went to see the cemetery,*[53] *it was formerly a stone quarry, but the rock is hollowing out into subterraneous apartments for the dead, & the lower part is converted into a garden. It is 3 years since it has been begun, but it is not yet finished.*

We neglected to say that in the morning, we went across the Mersey with papa,[54] *and returned again, in the same steam boat before 8 O'clock, on our return a steam-boat called the St George passed us, & arriving at the pier before us, fastened her rope, the mail being in our boat, when we came up, our captain called to the St George to move, but not yet having landed all her passengers, she would not stir, in consequence of which, we drove our prow against her stern scopped out some splinters of wood, & broke our own flag staff.*

18 June, Friday, Liverpool   *The next forenoon, we took a walk through Liverpool, and after dinner we left for Preston where we arrived about 9 O'clock.*[55]

19 June, Saturday, Preston   *Preston is a very nice clean town, situated on the banks of the river Ribble.*

20 June, Sunday, Preston   *The next day being Sunday, we went to the church which was close to the inn. the preacher had a beautiful voice, but the sermon was nothing particular. we had a very pleasant walk in the afternoon to the banks of the river.*

21 June, Monday, Preston   *[W]e left next morning about 10 for Kendal. the morning was very fine, tho' rather cold, we changed horses at Garstang,*[56] *& saw its castle from the road. The view from the hill above Lancaster*[57] *is extremely fine, the sun shone upon the ocean, which lay stretched like a mirror below us, while the distant cloud capped summits of the mountains on the opposite shore with Lancaster Castle towering in the foreground formed a* *lovely scene.*

We took a walk round the Castle while dinner was preparing, it is a fine old building, but part of it has been lately repaired, from the terrace which surrounds it we had again a beautiful view of the sea, together with the mountains, we left Lancaster about 4 O'clock, having many beautiful views of the hills,

Kendal[58] is very <beautifully> finely situated, in a large valley surrounded by lofty mountains, it was late when we arrived, &

22 June, Tuesday, Kendal   [W]e left early the next morning so that

we did not see much of the town, the next day we went to low wood inn[59] which is situated on the banks of Winandermere,

[S]oon after we arrived we took a walk on the shore of the Lake & coming to a convenient point, we tried to sail a little boat, but the string not having been firmly tied it gave way, & we soon had the pleasure of seeing our little boat, set off on its first voyage, Papa immediately ran back to the pier for a boat; While we remained watching the little runaway, they had considerable difficulty in finding it, after they had got it, they pulled in to the point where we stood & we leaping in, promised ourselves a delightful sail to the pier, but alas, the envious tricks of misfortune!   scarcely had we set off, before it began to rain heavily, & we crouching together under a pent house of umbrellas, we could not enjoy our sail, so much as we otherwise would have done,   we amused ourselves on the banks of the lake, till dinner time after which we took a Walk, in order to see the beautiful water-fall at Ambleside.[60]

[T]he road winds along the boarder of the lake & every here & there, from some opening between the trees, we had a most beautiful view, to the right were Langdale Pikes, & in the distance, Skaw-fell rears his giant bulk, having arrived at Ambleside we went through the yard of the Saluation Inn, & thence proceeded by the side of a stream as clear as crystal by a mountain path. after walking about ¾ of a mile, we found ourselves on the brink of a precipice, with the waterfall[61] to the right. it is partly hid by trees, which have overgrown the cliffs on both sides, it is divided into two parts by a rock in the centre, the rock is about   feet, over which it hurls itself, in masses of waving foam & sparkling spray, at the bottom is a sort of bason, from which it falls, forming another small cascade,   near Ambleside is the house of Mr Wordsworth,[62]   we got to low Wood, again about 7 O'clock, & did not go out any more that evening,

23 June, Wednesday, Low Wood   [T]he next morning before

breakfast, we had a very pleasant sail on the lake, it was a delightful morning, & it was wonderfull to observe the various shades thrown by the clouds on the mountains, which rested on their lofty summit while the lake glittered in the sunbeam like so many diamonds, after breakfast we had two other sails,

[W]e left Low-Wood about 12 O'clock, for Keswick, and stopt at Grasmere,[63] for two or three hours, while there we went to the top of a small hill[64] from which we had a fine view,   we left Grasmere about 4 O'clock,[65] and soon came in sight of Helvellyn which rises majestically from the banks of lake Thirlmere to the height of 3070 feet, above the level of the sea. On the opposite side are numerous beautiful crags, which at the time we saw them, glanced in the Sunbeams, & appeared like so many little streams of water gushing down their rocky summits, the scene was lovely, the glassy waters of Thirlmere, reflected the mountains above like the smoothest mirror, so that instead of looking into a lake, it appeared, as if we were looking down into a deep dell, so plainly were they reflected.

After gazing some time, on this enchanting scene, we pursued our rout to Keswick, the summit of Helvellyn was still seen towering above the neighbouring mountains for some time, after we descended the hill, which hid lake Thirlmere from our sight, in our rout we passed thro' St John's vale,[66] which is very beautiful, but still is nothing when compared with the beautiful vale of Keswick,[67] which we soon after came in view of, on ascending the hill above the town, that lovely valley burst upon our sight, in all its native grandeur, to the right the majestic Skiddaw[68] reared his double summit to the heavens, while the lovely Derwent lay stretched at our feet beautifully dotted with (green) islands, & to the extreme right was Saddle back,   having descended the hill, was the village of Keswick,[69] which is a small hamlet, about a quarter of a mile from the lake,

24 June, Thursday, Keswick   The next day we had a delightful

walk first to the lake, after which we ascended a small eminence on the Borrowdale road, called Castle Hill,[70] from which we had a beautiful view of the vale of Keswick, with the lakes of Derwent & Bassenthwaite, the latter of which was about 5 miles from Keswick, when we descended, the day had become so extremely hot, that we were very glad to get in to the hotel,

25 June, Friday, Keswick   [T]he next day being showry we went to

the museum[71] belonging to Mr Crosthwaite, son of the original founder when we entered the first thing that saluted our ears was the sound of an Eolian harp,[72] the second that of a tremendous gong,[73] which filled the room, with its most disagreeable noise, this instrument consists of a sort of iron plate peirced full of the smallest holes, which were almost invisible when struck, the iron vibrates in a most wonderful manner,   at one of the windows were two small heathen Gods, most ludicrous figures, which the natives carve out of wood, with their own hands, we saw a peice of the finest plumbago,[74] from the Borrowdale mines *value £2-5. also some wonderful petrifications, of tropical plants, found in this Country at the depth of between 50 and 60 feet, under ground as a leave of the prickly pear, 2 bamboo canes &c.* There were several old manuscript books, written before printing was invented, there was an immense bone, rather more than 1 yard & ¾, said to be the rib of a man, 21 feet high!! we saw a beautiful diamond beetle, in a glass. we also saw a very curious glass, which when we stood at a certain distance from it, we appeared to shake hands with our own shadow, there were a set of musical stones, which Mr Crosthwaite played a tune on, with a hammer, which were picked up, on the bed of the river Greta,[75] also a pair of shoes, which were said to be identical ones in which King Charles was beheaded, we were then shown the head of a New Zealand chief, & several other curiosities,

26 June, Saturday, Keswick   [T]he next morning (Saturday) being very wet, we did not go out, but the evening proving fine, we had a pleasant walk to the boarder of the lake.

27 June, Sunday, Keswick   On Sunday we went to Crosthwaite Church,[76] which is about a mile from the town of Keswick, we were put in a seat, that would have been a disgrace to any church, it was so dirty but we easily put up with that as in the seat directly opposite Mr Southey[77] sat We saw him very nicely   he seemed extremely attentive & by what we saw of him we should think him very pious. he has a very keen eye & looks extremely like — a poet. We had a very pleasant walk in the afternoon.

28 June, Monday, Keswick   On Monday we took a trip to Buttermere. Having procured an open carriage with two ponies following we set off[78] Our road lay along the banks of Derwent water And passing by the fall of Lowdore[79] we entered the straits of Borrowdale. This is an immense valley lying north & south receiving the head of Derwent water at its northern extremity which is called the straits of Borrowdale from its being much narrower than the rest of the valley This part has a very fine effect when seen from the other end of the lake. Looking back Skiddaw towered over the fine expanse of Derwent water & the fine crags richly clothed with trees on the eastern side of the lake had a fine effect   passing through the straits of Borrowdale the giant form of Castle crag[80] appeared in front A Roman station was formerly erected upon this rock evidently to command the pass of Borrowdale

We now came in sight of Bowder stone[81] an immense fragment of rock which seems to have been detached from the hill above & to have fallen to its present situation it is so balanced that it resembles a ship standing on its keel. Its length is said to be 62 feet its circumference 84   its solidity is about 29,000 feet & its weight about 1771 tons,

[H]aving passed Bowder stone the valley widens & includes a small space of cultivated land through which the river Derwent flows It is a beautiful stream as clear & limpid as any river amongst the lakes although small The mountains in this part are not so stupendous & craggy as in the straits but still they are very fine although rather barren.

Turning to the right towards Seatoller the carriage road ceases & we left our carriage which was to return & meet us at Buttermere[82] We then began to ascend the hill in a ravine by the side of a roaring torrent one of the sources of the Derwent The road was very steep and covered with loose stones many of which are a foot in diameter Every here & there a little streamlet crossed our path & joined the main torrent

The mountains here are extremely bold & precipitous Opposite were the celebrated mines for plumbago Proceeding onwards we came to Honistar Crag a tremendous precipice in which is a large slate quarry   it is almost quite perpendicular & has a very imposing effect. We then forded the river[83] & soon came in sight of Buttermere which though small is a very beautiful Lake. Red pike rises on the western side   it is a very sharp point of rock near this is a waterfall called sour milk Gill It proceeds from a small tarn in the hollow of the mountain & were there a greater quantity of water would be finer than most of the waterfalls of the lakes As we proceeded along the banks of Buttermere[84] we saw the head of Crummock water separated from Buttermere by a small neck of cultivated land. The mountains here are very lofty & their cloudcapped summits are extremely sublime their sides towards the lake are very <sublime> precipitous

When we arrived at the inn[85] we were put into a very comfortable room, *the Landlady who came to cover the table displayed an assortment of books, drawings, Copybooks, footstools, tea-mats &c &c[86] which her daughter had just brought from boarding-school, shortly after dinner[87] time, we set out, on our way home, we ascended[88] a very steep hill, which the ladies walked up, while the gentlemen rode on horseback, we had a very wet ride home, arrived there safely about 9 O'clock, we never enjoyed our tea more, and gladly retired in order to pay a visit to Morpheus, who entertained us very handsomely all night,*

29 *June, Tuesday, Keswick*   [T]*he next day we were to have ascended Skiddaw, but it was so very wet, that we could not get out all day, —*

30 June, Wednesday, Keswick   [T]*he following day*, proving fine we laid in a good store of sandwiches & brandy & having procured four ponies set off on the ascent of that celebrated mountain[89] We proceeded a little way on the road to Penrith then striking to the left we wound round the base of Latrigg which is a green hill about a thousand feet high at the base of Skiddaw[90]

Just before we got to that mountain there was a bog through which we had to force our horses   having struggled through it we came to the base of Skiddaw itself   we then began to ascend the steepest part of the mountain   every here & there was a step of about a foot high consisting of large stones   having got up this we came to a nearly level part of the mountain covered with rich velvety turf. here in a small hollow is a fine spring of water[91] where we refreshed ourselves for the last toilsome ascent which is nearly as steep as that we had already got over. This brought us to the highest summit seen from Keswick[92] from which we had to proceed along a ridge of Loose shingly slate to the highest point of the mountain on which is a high heap of stones from the top of which caring not for the wind which now was a pretty brisk gale we gazed at the astonishing prospect which lay stretched beneath our feet.[93]

Looking westward we thought we could discern the hills of the Isle of Man but of this we could not be certain. South the crags of Borrowdale were tossed in wild but majestic confusion & in the back ground Scawfell reared his gigantic head   the monarch of the mountains and the scene was <clothed> closed by the summit of Coniston old man but the guides were not quite certain that it was that mountain   Keswick & Derwent water were hid from us by the second summit of the mountain   south east was seen the enormous bulk of Helvellyn & the whole range of that name was plainly discernable. But we could not see Ullswater or Placefell as Helvellyn interposed itself between us and those objects   east the barren moors around Penrith were Discernible with two small hills called the lesser & greater Mellfell But great part of the country in that quarter was shut out by the huge head of Saddleback & north <was> were the sands of the Solway frith with a wide range of Scottish hills beyond   The high head of Ingleborough was faintly seen to the southeast by <east> south

[H]aving surveyed this wild prospect with great delight we dismounted from out <steeds> horses & descended the mountain without difficulty the whole time we had occupied being about 6 hours. We were very fortunate in the day as we might have gone up a hundred times & and not have had the view we had that day.

1 July, Thursday, Keswick   The next morning we left Keswick in order to go to Patterdale at the head of Ullswater.[94] we wound along the base of Saddleback which is a most beautiful and majestic mountain intersected by deep ravines The day was beautiful and we had a delightful prospect The view behind us was bounded by Grasmoor and the surrounding mountains The craggy summits of the Helvellyn range appeared on our right And the distant <summits> hills of Shapfell were feintly distinguished on the eastern horizon.

Leaving Saddleback we passed by a small hill called Mellfell and came in sight of a craggy & enormous mountain which we thought must be Helvellyn but we were not sure After proceeding a little way further and ascending the brow of a hill, we had the first view of Ullswater We were much struck with the first view of the Lake which bore a totally different character from any other we had hitherto visited as it combined the beauties of them all. The opposite shore was indeed a scene of mountain grandeur as the cliffs seemed nearly to overhang the lake so perpendicularly did they rise from its waters.

When we reached the bottom of the hill we walked a short distance to Lyulphs tower[95] which is a small fortification on the banks of the lake erected for a hunting box <by admiral> From it we had a very nice view of the lake both up & down We then returned to the carriage and wound along the shore of the lake every opening affording us a different view. The wind was rather high and the lake being a good deal ruffled it looked like the sea itself. We passed by the palace of the king of Patterdale[96] which is a nice house belonging to Mr [Marshall] so called from being the richest gentleman and possessing the most land of any in the dale.

The end of the lake which we had now reached partook more of the softness of Windermere that of its own bold & romantic character but still it is very grand and the towering place fell is an extremely striking mountain

The inn[97] is within sight of the lake   that is it is possible to see a very small portion of the ugliest part of it and it is at least half a mile from it   in the evening we had a very pleasant walk on the banks of the lake[98]

2 July, Friday, Patterdale   In the morning just before we set out for Lowwood[99] we were told that there was a most dangerous most difficult & most fatiguing hill to be ascended & that it was utterly

impossible to think of ascending that same hill unless we took with us
four horses   at first we were determined that we would not do so &
at last they were determined that we should do so so we were forced to
take that number to the top of the hill which we found very insignificant to what we had been led to expect   When we reached the top
we had a fine view of the head of Windermere & the surrounding
country   We then descended a much worse hill than we had
ascended and found ourselves at Ambleside from whence we had a
pleasant ride to Lowwood[100]

3 July, Saturday, Low Wood   <The day after we after

arrived> The day after we arrived we intended to have a fishing
expedition   And accordingly after breakfast although the day was
far from promising we stepped into the boat for that purpose   But
scarcely were we <scarcely were we> seated rightly before a most
provoking shower of rain drove us in again <for that>   A second
time we put off to sea & a second time we were driven in   a third
trial was attended with the same bad success   Still not daunted by
our continued defeats a fourth time we tried the combat reached the
point we wished and threw out our lines   there we lay for half an
hour without a bite   I drew up my rod. No bait was visible   it was
baited again & thrown into the water   A drop of rain ruffled the
glassy surface of the water   down came another   in a few minutes
all traces of blue sky were lost & we were nobly peppered ere we
reached home without either bite or fish   thus ended our fishing
expedition

4 July, Sunday, Low Wood   The next morning being Sunday

we went to Rydal Chapel[101] in preference to Ambleside as we heard
that Mr Wordsworth[102] went to Rydal which is a most beautiful little
chapel built by Lady Fleming The windows were executed with none of
the modern finery but yet with great chasteness & elegance   the
pulpit was neatly although plainly carved and altogether it was one of
the most beautiful little chapels we ever saw
    We were lucky in procuring a seat very near that of Mr Words-
worth, *there being only one between it, & the one we were in*, We were rather
disappointed in this gentlemans appearance [this word is written by
Ruskin in a back-hand] especially as he appeared asleep the greatest
part of the time   He <appeared> seemed about 60   This gentleman possesses a long face and a large nose with a moderate assortment
of grey hairs and 2 small grey eyes not filled with fury wrapt inspired

with a mouth of moderate dimensions that is quite large enough to let in a sufficient quantity of beef or mutton & to let out a sufficient quantity of poetry

In the afternoon we walked up a trifling hill in order to obtain a fine view   We exercised our eyes well on this occasion as the day before papa had with considerable difficulty killed a very venomous snake as it was crawling across this walk   We all acknowledged this view to be the finest we had seen of the lake for we saw nearly the whole of it with all the islands.

On our return we met with an old man who called himself the poet of these lakes[103] He repeated some of his verses to us and said that he would have been the finest poet of the lakes if he had had a leeberal edication He had a fine countenance but his verses were but so so   We had a very pleasant walk home

5 July, Monday, Low Wood   On Monday morning shortly
after breakfast we set out in a boat to visit the station about 5 miles from lowwood   We had a very pleasant sail down the lake and landed on an island belonging to Mr Curwen[104] & on which he had a house It is the largest [island] in the lake being about a mile long   We then crossed to the other side of the Island where we found our boat waiting us when we again embarked and landed at the ferry house[105] which is a small inn just below the station & walked to that place which also belongs to Mr Curwen

It is a large tower in which is a large apartment with various painted windows   The people tell you that on looking through the light blue it represents the appearance of winter. The green represents spring   the yellow summer   the purple a thunderstorm and the orange autumn   Each window of this place presented a different prospect of the lake and all were equally beautiful

Here there was a sage Nestor of a dog about 11 years old   He was not wanting in hoary hairs as his colour was white and brown   Altogether he had a very wise & venerable appearance & we all gave him a pat which he was graciously pleased to acknowledge by a wag of his tail

On leaving the station we re-entered our boat & crossed the lake to Bowness a beautiful little village situated on the Border of the lake   The village itself is much more beautiful than the bay on which it is situated as the beach is not wanting in dead cats & dogs & the water is dirty from the quantity of boats continually sailing about the bay and when they land ploughing up the sand at the bottom with their keels   Having looked a little about Bowness we again entered our boat & returned to Lowwood.

We heard that there was to be a boatrace[106] upon the lake that afternoon from the waterhead to the station & back again   We saw the boats pass (of which there were only two with four rowers in each) while we were at dinner & some time afterwards we set out in a boat to see the conclusion of the race   We lay to for some time till we saw the boats appear & then began to pull slowly towards the waterhead. One boat which was beautifully shaped beat the other by nearly a quarter of a mile

6 July, Tuesday, Low Wood   The next morning we proposed to go to Coniston and being informed that there would be no rain that day we accordingly set off for that place

We proceeded about 5 miles when we reached the ferry[107] where there was a very large boat   The horses 1st entered & were first tied up to one end The carriage was next with some difficulty rolled after them & last of all we followed. This sail was not quite so agreeable as some others that we had had   However we got over without any terrible misfortune & landed safely on the other side.[108] where we walked up a very steep & long hill & then down again on the other side when contrary to the prophesies of the good people of Lowwood who trusting to their own judgement had begun to cut their hay it came on to rain and before we reached Coniston it became a settled rainy day. This was a terrible disappointment but we bore it with uncommon fortitude.

It cleared up for a few minutes when we availed ourselves of the opportunity & took a turn near the door. However the window of our room looked upon the lake the shore of which was only the breadth of the road from the inn & we made the best use of our window & also of our eyes in contemplating this beautiful lake with its surrounding hills

Coniston water is about 6 miles long   It is a very fine lake but there is only one mountain in its vicinity Namely Coniston Old Man about 2200 feet high[109] but the higher part of the mountain was so concealed by mist that we could not distinguish it from lower & less celebrated mountains. This mountain contains several rich copper mines.

We had some very fine char for dinner.[110] This fish is <caught in only> peculiar to a few of the Lakes in Westmoreland & Cumberland. The largest are caught in Coniston but they are equally fine in Winandermere, those we had were of a light salmon colour & tasted like salmon trout.

Although it was a wet day we enjoyed ourselves very much and about five o'clock we set off on our return to Lowwood. We returned home by the head of the lake at Ambleside.[111] We had a very pleasant ride & enjoyed our tea exceedingly –

7, 8, 9 July, Wednesday, Thursday, Friday, Low Wood   The three following days we did nothing in particular but had many pleasant little sails & other enjoyments.

10 July, Saturday, Low Wood   On Saturday we left Lowwood intending to spend our Sunday at Bowness before mentioned.[112] While dinner was preparing we walked up to Biscuit Holme[113] which is a small hill above Bowness where we had a fine view of the lake with all its Islands. We did not find Bowness quite so agreeable as Low-wood but we had a very pleasant sail towards Newby Bridge[114]

11 July, Sunday, Bowness   On Sunday we went to the church[115] which was close to the inn. We were put into a very cold seat which [was] directly opposite the door & behind the pulpit, *so that we would hardly hear a word, After service we walked to   Bank,[116] about two miles from Bowness, where we had the finest view of the Lake, which we had hither to seen, except that above Low-wood, but while we were (surveying) admiring the beauties of the scene* a heavy shower of rain came on which obliged us to scamper home in the best way & as soon as we possibly could

12 July, Monday, Bowness   We left Bowness[117] about 10 O clock on Monday morning & with the greatest regret bade farewell to the lakes, *we shortly arrived in Kendal, where we stayed till the next morning; in the afternoon, we took a walk to the Castle,[118] which looks very well from the town, but is a disagreeable nettly place, when you are at it.*

13 July, Tuesday, Kendal   [W]e *left Kendal early on Tuesday morning, which was very fine, and we enjoyed the ride very much to Kirkby Lonsdale where we breakfasted,[119] while breakfast was getting ready, we took a short walk to the Churchyard, where we had a most beautiful view of the river, & the surrounding Country;[120]   after breakfast we walked to the river side in order to see a most beautiful bridge which the good inhabitants of Kirkby Lonsdale, not knowing the builder of, have ascribed to his Black Majesty;[121] it is one of the most beautiful bridges we ever saw,* Certainly whoever was the author of it he certainly has chosen a most uncouth place for its foundation   It seems to be the most rocky part of the river   the rocks are very peculiarly formed lying in regular laminal shelving down to the water which is of a deep brown from rising among the peat mosses & the very foam with which it is partially covered from dashing among the rocks is of a brown tinge   It is a very good fishing river

We returned home by a different path & immediately set off for Lancaster[122] where we arrived to dinner; *while dinner was getting ready, we took a short walk into the Country after which we ascended the Castlehill, which we were as much pleased with as before, immediately after dinner we proceeded to Preston by way of Garstang,   the afternoon was delightful, and we had a very pleasant ride,*

[W]hen we arrived within a few miles of the destined conclusion of our day's journey, we were somewhat astounded, by observing an immense number of Horses, Dogs Carriages Gigs, Carts, Irish Sociables, Cars, Donkey's & men, <indeed it is almost useless to name them both, as one Epithet will express both their qualities> all <these> coming from the same place viz – the race course,[123] & going different ways, we could hardly get thro' the town, the number of people was so great,

[H]aving struggled through this formidable phalanx we arrived at our old friend the black Bull and were somewhat astounded at the most appalling intelligence that they had not beds enough for the party unless a gentleman went away by the coach that very identical evening And in case that coverance should by any unfortunate & unforeseen chance be full what alas should be done with us, *but fortune proved favourable to us, the mail was not full, & so we were all accommodated*

Lord Derby,[124] with some other gentlemen dined in the inn, so there was nothing but bustle from the time we went in till the time we came out,

14 July, Wednesday, Preston   [W]e left Preston at 7 O'clock next

morning for Manchester, we breakfasted at Yarrow bridge which is a nice little inn[125] between Chorley & Bolton, & about 10 miles from Preston; we arrived in Manchester about one oclock we took a walk thro' this town in the afternoon,

15 July, Thursday, Manchester   & left it next morning about 7,

in order to proceed to Castleton,

[W]e passed thro' Stockport & from thence to Disley,[126] a small village between that town and Chapel en le frith, while we were at Breakfast, we saw four horses waiting for a stage, one of which ran away, which afforded us a little amusement for a time, but it was soon damped by hearing that the poor horse had fallen down in running & broken its legs so severely, that it was obliged to be *shot directly* and we soon heard the report of the gun.

We soon set off for Castleton & passing through Chapel en le Frith ascending a steep long hill & descending again on the other side by the base of Mam Tor hereafter mentioned we arrived there[127] to dinner & were put into a nice room with a fine bow window

16 July, Friday, Castleton   The next morning we set off in order to explore the peak Cavern[128] to its end   A <little way> short distance from the inn we came to the banks of a streamlet which proceeded from the cave. Going along its banks we entered the narrow ravine at the end of which the cave appears   This glen is very narrow & the rocks on both sides are extremely high & perpendicular. A projecting rock hides the entrance to the cavern until you are close to it when turning the point it bursts upon you with the greatest grandeur   The arch is extremely high & the sight of the immense hollow within is very striking

In the entrance there are several poor people who make cord twine &c   They strongly reminded us of the shades plying their eternal tasks in the regions of darkness

Keeping to the right we proceeded onwards a few yards when we came to a large mass of rock in the middle of the path. Here a candle was given to each & still keeping to the right we came to a small door the true entrance to the cavern   Here we were desired to look back to the entrance when the effect of daylight through the arch was very surprising.

Passing through the door the rocks became so low that we were obliged to stoop our heads in order to avoid striking them against the roof   We then came to the Bellhouse a small cavern so called from there being several holes in the roof of the form of a bell   2 of these are nearly completely circular.

Thence again stooping we came to the edge of the little river Styx as it is called. This is a small water about a foot & a half deep & a few yards broad   here there was what was called a boat but it far more resembled a pickling tub, *two of us were directed to* enter this & to lie down when the guide stepped into the water & wading by the side of the boat pushed us along to the other side where landing we waited till the rest of the party were ferried over.

We then found ourselves in what was called Plutos hall which is the longest cavern to be seen but as our eyes were not yet accustomed to darkness we could not view it so well   Still proceeding onwards we came to the chancel and thence through Roger Rains house to the devils cellar From which there was a long passage sometimes lower & sometimes higher which brought us into a cavern called Great tom of Lincoln from which a shorter passage brought us to the end of this vast cavern   we then began to retrace our steps & entered great Tom of Lincoln   This cavern although not large is remarkable for its shape as it materially resembles a bell.

Thence we proceeded on by the banks of a beautiful stream which flows through the greatest part of the cavern this we frequently crossed. The rocks were sometimes so low that we were obliged to stoop considerably but in most places we could stand upright

We then entered a cavern which we had not before seen It was very high but it was also very narrow. Here our guide ascended to the top by means of pieces of wood fixed in the rock & lighted a Bengal light   this produced a very curious effect as we could see the roof of the cavern very distinctly   The guide asked us if we would like to hear a blast   But we declined it & went on guided by a little girl whilst he remained behind with another gentleman in order to let him hear it. We followed the little girl till we were at a sufficient distance from the place where the gunpowder was put   She then left us and we waited until the gentleman and guide came up to contemplate the chasm we were in

Here the stream disappears & seems to thunder into an immense gulf below. we held our candles above our heads in order to see the place where it disappeared more distinctly. It appeared to be a hole about 3 feet in diameter. but we could see no more as all beyond was darkness. We then proceeded to the devils cellar. This [is] a large cavern but there was a sort of division in the roof that made it appear double,

[T]hence we went to Roger Rain's house, a small cavern so called from a quantity of water always trickling down in one part, this whether summer or winter is never dry. we next entered the chancel, which is a very large cavern, there is a chasm in the top, in which a few years ago, several musicians were placed, who when any persons, visited the cave, played a few tunes, which must have re-echoed through the cave, in a very beautiful manner, this chasm was lighted up, by several candles, and showed us the whole of the cavern, which was extremely sublime,

[W]e then re-entered Pluto's hall, which is the largest of the caverns, and our eyes having become accustomed to the darkness, we had a much finer view of it than on our first entrance, especially as it was now well lighted up it was very grand & solemn We then recrossed the water & passing through the bell house we came to the door mentioned[129]

the other side at the bottom was Satan dragging the wicked into hell, and grinning horribly a Ghastly smile. Lightning was seen striking them down. Magdalen College library was a very pleasant room, with a good many books in it. at one end was a most beautiful picture of our Saviour bearing his cross. it was long supposed to have been painted by Guido but lately ascertained to have been done by Morelles. Leaving Magdalen College we went to Christchurch & saw the large hall where the students dine. There were ninetynine pictures amongst which were those of Henry the 8th Cardinal Wolsey & Mr Canning & Doctor Busby of flogging memory &c That afternoon we went to the waterside to see the students rowing in jumping out of a boat one nearly fell into the water but he escaped. The next day we took a walk in the town & danced into the courts of almost all the colleges but always danced out again without seeing anything worthy of being put down In the evening we saw some Morrice dancers The next day we left Oxford & got to Blenheim to breakfast We then went to see the duke of Marlborough's house There were a great many invaluable pictures By Rubens Guido Carlo Dolce Teniers Rembrandt Sir Joshua Reynolds & many others There was one picture of Charles the 1st on horseback which was pronounced by Sir Joshua Reynolds to be the finest equestrian piece he had ever seen. There was also a most beautiful picture by Carlo Dolce & a very fine Bacchanalian piece by Rubens. there was a very pleasing picture of the late Duke & Duchess

1   Page 3 of the manuscript

2 The Baskerville family travelling chariot, early 19th century

3 Christ Church Chapel (Oxford Cathedral), drawing by John Ruskin, 1838

4   Warwick Castle, drawing by John Ruskin, 1847

5 Street scene in Derby, drawing by John Ruskin, 1837

6 Langdale Pikes over Windermere from Low Wood, 1837

7 Coniston Hall and Old Man from Brantwood, 1837

8   Haddon Hall, drawing by John Ruskin, 1838

9   Gloucester Cathedral, drawing by John Ruskin, ?1834

The door was opened when one of us was admitted & the door immediately shut again   The effect of the daylight was astonishing. The leaves of the bushes outside the cavern had a very singular appearance seen through the immense concave. And the sun shining bright when we re-entered the open air enlivened us very much. After entering a small room belonging to the guide & putting down our names[130] as is the custom we returned home

Shortly after we set out to visit the Speedwell mine[131] after walking about a mile we came to a small cottage the residence of the guide   We descended 106 steps & then came to the water along which we were to be conducted. We got into a large boat just large enough to go along the passage which was upwards of 700 yards long   it was all blown out of solid rock   It resembled a pipe partly filled with water which was about four feet deep   The miners were eleven years in blowing it out of the rock

[H]aving arrived at the end we landed & found ourselves in an enormous cavern. On our left was a tremendous gulph which is unfathomable   several thousand tons of rubbish have been thrown into this chasm without any perceptible alteration in its depth   the top is so very high that no light can reach it. A Bengal light being placed about 8 feet down the chasm we gazed into the immense abyss and the guide turned a sluice which let a greater quantity of water fall into it which made a prodigious noise falling from such a tremendous height   Another Bengal light was also placed *in the higher part of the cavern which gave us a slight idea of the immense vacuity of the place, after gazing around us for some time at this stupendous work of nature, we re-entered our boat,   it was not quite so cold coming back, as going, the <ceiling> roof was so low, in some parts, that we were obliged to stoop a little, at least those who were on the side had,   of all the horrible <things> places, we had ever been in, this was the most horrible,   we were very glad to find ourselves once more in the open air, & at a pleasant distance from the Devil's Hall (the name of the Cavern).*

In the afternoon, we procured a vehicle, which conducted us to the foot of Mam-tor,[132] or the Shivering mountain,   the ascent is very steep, but exceedingly pleasant,   we were surprised to find that this mountain to its very summit, was covered with fine rich velvety turf,   it was a beautiful afternoon but rather windy, from the top we had a fine prospect of Eder dale, as well as Hope Dale, the latter is far the most extensive, but the former is thought the most beautiful, on account of its having more wood,   we descended by a more easy path, & returned home by the Winnets a most romantic glen a little to the west of Castleton   One of the rocks so very much resembles a square tower so much so that at the top of Mam tor we mistook it for one   Altogether this ravine was more beautiful although not so stupendous & striking as even Borrowdale.

17 July, Saturday, Castleton   On the next morning we took a

ride to Sheffield[133] which is 16 miles from Castleton Part of the road lies through Hope dale & is very good but the rest is hilly & the country is very barren

Sheffield is a large and smoky town from the number of manufactories   while we were there [we] went to see Rogers & Sons[134] show rooms   There were a great many handsome pieces of workmanship amongst which was a knife containing 1821 blades besides other instruments   It was a most awful most fearful most repulsive & prodigious monstrous prodigy of cutlery   We also saw an exact resemblance of a knife presented to his late majesty George the 4th By Rogers and Sons at Carlton palace   also twelve pairs of Scissors quite perfect which altogether do not weigh one grain besides various other articles   Shortly afterwards we left Sheffield and arrived at Castleton about 4 oclock to dinner

18 July, Sunday, Castleton   The next day (Sunday) we went to

Hope Church[135] distant a mile and a half as Castleton church was undergoing repairs   We had a very good Sermon & the clergyman seemed a serious man   after returning from church we took a walk up to Peverils castle[136] which is a fine old ruin   on one side it is defended by the ravine at one end of which is the entrance of the cave   On the opposite side and back by another ravine   The front is the weakest part as the hill there is easily ascended but still it is very steep   The keep is the most perfect part not much overgrown   The walls are <about 5 feet thick> exceedingly thick   In them are the remains of a narrow staircase which seems to have led to the upper part of the tower   What remains of the walls still seemed very strong but a great part of them is fallen (Sir Walter Scott's son at Castleton)[137]   From the top we had a very extensive view of Hope dale Mam Tor & the surrounding hills

19 July, Monday, Castleton   Having heard that the Bradshaw

mine was more beautiful than any of the rest on Monday morning we set out for the purpose of seeing it   it[138] is situated in a field about 3 miles from Castleton   On arriving there the Guide brought an old miners coat and hat for each of us from which we suspected that there was something to be gone through not quite agreeable and after much laughter at the figures which we presented we began to descend   the cave was so narrow that we continuously rubbed ourselves against the wet rock on each side and now & then we were obliged to stoop

After descending about half of the way papa looked up and saw that we were in a most dangerous situation. The mine consisted of a vein of Lead Ore about 2 feet wide which had been worked in a perpendicular direction by the miners till they came to the natural cavern   In order to descend this the miners had formed artificial steps which consisted of large & loose stones merely supported by branches of trees fixed into the rock on both sides which must be continually getting more & more rotten by the droppings of water

When the steps had gone down a certain *distance they suddenly turned so that the steps we had descended, were above our heads, should one of the branches give way the stones which it supported must fall upon the stairs below, which giving way under the pressure, would have borne down all the understeps, thus leaving an* unconquerable obstacle between us and the entrance   No sooner did we see this than we hurried up as fast as we could at the risk of having all the steps about our ears Glad were we when we again saw the light of day & threw off our musty fusty dusty rusty coats

The old man followed muttering all manner of persuasions to make us risk our precious lives by entering his precious cave <However the guide> He said that he was a proverb of timidity & in order to prove it he went down this hole several times a day at the danger of cracking still more his already cracked skull   However all his persuasions were lost upon us for we got into our vehicle and trotted home as fast as we could and on reaching the inn we immediately set off for Matlock

We intended dining at Bakewell which is about 10 miles from Matlock[139] and looking a little about a place but just as we got there it began to rain, so as it was out of the question seeing anything of <Matlock> Bakewell we determined to proceed to our old friend Matlock where we arrived to dinner & were somewhat pleased to see again the noble *cliffs & their leafy clothing*

20 July, Tuesday–2 August, Monday, Matlock   As [we had already] *seen all the principal places & things, & as the weather was so excessively warm that we could not go out but in the evening, we saw nothing new. A friend[140] having come on a visit to us for a few days who had been four years absent from England, we took a ride one morning to Bakewell to*

breakfast[141] *It was a most beautiful morning & the road from Matlock to Bakewell is very pretty so we all enjoyed our ride exceedingly*

[A]*fter breakfast we* visited Chatsworth house which we found standing just as it stood before   we were quite as much if not more delighted with the house than we were before but were told to our extreme mortification that the copper tree would be ready to play in a few hours   Alas a few hours were to us the same as a few years   we could not stay   We then returned to Bakewell where we dined & then visited Haddon Hall & from thence returned home to tea which we rather enjoyed after our thirty miles journey.

On Sat[urday] evening we went to Stoness[142] we spent our fortnight <at Matlock> very delightfully & it was with great regret that we bade farewell for a time to Matlock

2 August, Monday, Matlock   We went to Ashbourne which is 14 miles from Matlock to breakfast[143] Soon after breakfast we went to see the cathedral[144] in which is a very beautiful monument[145] erected to the memory of Penelope only daughter of Sir & Lady Brook Boothby executed by   This child who died at 6 years old is represented like those at Lichfield as lying upon a couch   And the celebrated Chantry is said to have taken the idea of that at Lichfield from this monument   Upon the tomb is a simple epitaph in these words   The unfortunate parents ventured their all upon this frail bark & the wreck was total   (Horse & cart run away at Wolverhampton)[146] We then returned to the inn & shortly after set off

We went by Uttoxeter Stafford Penkridge Wolverhampton Stourbridge and from thence to Bromsgrove where we slept having travelled nearly 80 miles in the course of the day[147]

3 August, Tuesday, Bromsgrove   We intended next morning to go through <Esham> Eves[ham] but were deterred from our purpose by hearing that they would have no horses there as an election was going on and so we went through Tewkesbury & Gloucester to Cheltenham where we arrived to dinner[148] Shortly after we agreed for lodgings directly opposite the plough[149] which we took possession of next morning after breakfast

4 August, Wednesday–17 August, Wednesday, Cheltenham   The first evening we took a walk in the Montpellier Gardens[150] which are the most resorted to   There is a large ball room & a rotunda, *in which the waters are drunk this is very handsomely lighted up, in*

the evening, there is a regular band which play, all the year morning &
evening, at which time a great many people walk,   there is a broad walk
about 150 feet in length, but rather confined from the <trees having> hedge
being too high; Near the Montpellier on the opposite side of the Turnpike road is
the Royal Well,[151] so called from George the Third's drinking of its waters when
at Cheltenham, the walk consists of a beautiful avenue, of the tallest poplars we
have ever seen, opposite the pump Room, is a small building where the waters
were formerly given out,   it is square,   on every side there is an arch,
which is filled with wire work, (small) close enough to keep in small birds, of
which there are a great number inside amongst which is the red headed
woodpecker, the drollest little bird we ever saw,   there is also a beautiful pair
of turtle doves, a partridge, a Blackbird, thrushes, with a variety of Canaries,
Bullfinches, Goldfinches, & other birds,   there is also another spa called the
imperial or Sherbourne,[152] but this is not much frequented, A spa has lately been
built by a private Gentleman, called the Pittville,[153] this altho' not the most
frequented, is the handsomest of them all, <there> it has a great deal more
ground than the others, & it has a small piece of water on which there are
several boats, The room is also much larger, there are several large & handsome
pillars between the rotunda & ballroom, it commands an extensive country but
more particularly so <from> when you look out of the upper windows, to which
you ascend by a flight of stairs, which bring you into a gallery which is carried
round the ball room from which you enter two apartments, which are as yet not
appropriated to any particular use.

We remained here a fortnight & walked morning & evening when
the weather permitted. One evening while we were there there was a
beautiful exhibition of fireworks which we went to see & enjoyed very
much. What added very much to the gaiety of the place was the
presence of his Royal Highness the Duke of Gloucester[154] who walked
regularly & drank the waters every morning

One forenoon we had a ride to Gloucester[155] which is distant 9
miles from Cheltenham   We had a beautiful ride there as the day
was most delightful   Having arrived there we took a walk towards
the river to see the ships We then returned to the inn and after
lunching we set out in order to see the cathedral

Before the person came who was to show us the cathedral we
walked round it or rather half round hoping to get back to the front
again another way but were disappointed[156] The outside of this
cathedral is quite equal to the inside.[157] The whole of the work &
<indeed> particularly the top of the steeple is built in a style of
elegance which combines in it both beauty & strength & yet it is so light
so airy & seemingly so frail that it appears as if the 1st tempest which

past over it would hurl it into destruction & scatter its fragments to the wind & even the solid parts are so richly ornamented & carved that they convey to you the same idea

The niches & cornices of the buttresses were ornamented with very old & what have once been fine statues   But some of these having had the misfortune to lose their head and others their tail & a number more having been lost altogether   The places once occupied by them looked as comfortless cold and desolate as any bare stone niche could have been   In every part of the cathedral there were grotesque <faces> heads of all kinds & some <Virginei volucrum vultus foedissima ventrix probies uncaeque manus> new monster stared you in the face at every corner.

In a kind of yard at the back of the cathedral we observed some low arched Iron barred windows on a level with the ground & having a mind to see what was inside we went up & peered into them. It appeared to be a dark deep vault[158] the roof of which was on a level with the ground & supported by massive round saxon pillars some yards in circumference   The opposite end of the vault we could not see but the distance faded into darkness drear & even the dim outlines of the pillars could scarcely have been seen had they not been white mellowed by age into a light grey. It was a ghostly place   This vault or at least one which we supposed to be it will be spoken of hereafter.

We now returned to the front and the person who was to show us the cathedral having arrived we entered the massive gateways[159]   The 1st thing which struck [us] was the immense size of the massive Saxon pillars which support the body of the cathedral The saxon architecture having always a massive & solid effect in itself

These pillars appeared almost *more* vast and gigantic than they really were

On the lefthand side as you enter in the corner of the cathedral was a statue of the famous Doctor Jenner[160] who 1st introduced vaccination inoculation or some other botheration of the kind   He certainly has done a great deal of service to his country & is worthy of this monument

We walked up the aisle of the church admiring the numberless & various monuments with which it was adorned They were all elaborate specimens of sculpture & most of them worthy of the chisel of a Chantry or Westmacott or Canova but one among the many struck us particularly

The circumstances which gave rise to the conception was a lady with her child having been shipwrecked & both drowned[161] It was supposed to be the day of Judgement   The mothers [body] was rising from the waves which receding around her yielded up their prey with her infant in her arms   An Angel lent her his assisting hand while others fanning her with their balmy wings were about to conduct her to heaven   The spotless marble seemed not an unapt emblem of the pure spirit & the lifeless stone spoke to the very heart of the spectator and almost drew tears   Underneath were written those beautiful words from the Apocalypse[162]   And the sea gave up the dead which were in it   Altogether this monument was one of the most striking & interesting nature

There were a great many other monuments too numerous to be enumerated. Amongst these was a very ancient piece of sculpture[163] representing a very large family consisting of a father and mother with 9 sons & 7 daughters all in a kneeling position in regimental order   The ancients seem to have been very prolific   We seldom see such large marble families nowadays Or at least the ancients were very conceited for if there are such large families they do not perpetuate their memory in such style.

We next surveyed a long range of various chapels which were extremely ancient   They had all once been most beautifully carved and must have been the work of many years   the screens[164] which separated them from the main body of the cathedral consisted of light & beautiful arches in Gothic about a foot wide and of various height. The pillars between them were extremely thin & generally fluted or rather consisting of several very small pillars & embossed with various flowers ornaments and figures   In rows side by side in the walls were numerous niches which once had the honour of supporting figures of different saints & martyrs and the feet or heads of some actually remained   But O dear, Oliver Cromwell that beheader of kings that polluter of churches that devastator of kingdoms that destroyer of cities that burner of villages entered this peaceful shrine and and and
Need we say any more   completely defaced these ornaments
Even now the carving is eminently gloriously wonderfully astoundingly and astonishingly beautiful notwithstanding all the efforts that have been made to deface it

We next examined another part of the body of the cathedral very different but more beautiful less massive and more modern than the huge pillars formerly spoken of[165]   This alteration was made in consequence of an accident   Some time ago they contrived some how to manage so clumsily that they got this part of the cathedral set on fire and of course as is usual in such cases it was burnt down   Now as the good people of Gloucester knew that sitting with their hands before them and crying out Oh what a pity would do no good they determined forthwith to build it up again ——— But as they knew nothing of Saxon architecture & did not understand building such monsters of pillars they set about building it in their own way thinking it would make variety. So they did & accordingly these pillars were projected planned & built

We must now describe them   They were very lofty & appeared to consist of a great many small pillars put together and at the top branching lightly and beautifully off so that where the branches of two pillars met it formed the point of the Gothic arch   These pillars were extremely beautiful & we do not [think] that the Cathedral ultimately sustained any loss by the fire.

As we were returning to the entrance our guide informed us that underneath the pavement on which we were walking was a vault which contained a great many hundred cartloads of human bones[166]   This we suspected to be the vault we had seen on the outside

We then returned to the inn & our carriage being ready we set off for Cheltenham. We had a very pleasant
ride & arrived there to
dinner[167]

Notes

1. Their route from Herne Hill probably took them along Camberwell Road and Walworth Road to the Elephant and Castle, thence along Westminster Bridge Road and across Westminster Bridge. North of the Thames, they could have travelled by way of Birdcage Walk, Constitution Hill, and Hyde Park to Marble Arch, there emerging into the country and following a westerly course to Ealing.
2. No village or house called Uphall can be traced anywhere near the route at this point. However the road from Ealing to Uxbridge passes through Southall. It seems likely that John Ruskin wrote 'Uphall' in error for Southall.
3. At the time of Ruskin's visit, Gerrards Cross was a hamlet in the parish of Fulmer, not being created a separate parish until 1861. The inn at Gerrards Cross was the Bull. The 1830 Land Tax returns (Bucks County Archives Q/RP1/8/51) describe the inn as being owned by William Weller and in the occupation of Stephen Munten. Originally part of the Bulstrode Park Estate, the inn was built in the seventeenth century and underwent various extensions. The original timbered front was replaced by the present one in the early nineteenth century, so the building that Ruskin saw may have been very different in appearance to the Bull of today. The inn was not one of the regular stage coach stops but was popular with private travellers who did not want to put up at the busier

inns. It had stabling for thirty horses. The hotel now belongs to the De Vere Group.

The 'Duke of Portland's grounds' at Gerrards Cross is Bulstrode Park. The owner at the time of Ruskin's visit was the fourth duke. An earlier owner had been Judge Jeffreys. The famous Portland Vase had come to Bulstrode in the time of the second duke. The third duke was twice prime minister, and after the end of his second term of office in 1809 he made the house a centre of political activity. The house and estate now belong to the Worldwide Evangelization Crusade.

4. The route from Gerrards Cross to Oxford lay through Beaconsfield and High Wycombe, in all some 35 miles. In Oxford they probably stayed at the Angel, 84 High Street. It was a large inn, now gone, on the south side nearly opposite Queen's College. Ruskin and his father stayed there in October 1836 when Ruskin matriculated as a Gentleman Commoner. In a rhyming letter to Richard Fall (*Works* II: 472) Ruskin wrote,

> The 'Angel' was our choice – we always went
> To that – we like an old establishment.

5. In 1877 Ruskin wrote to Susan Beever (*Works* XXXVII: 234) 'You know the *cathedral* of Oxford is the chapel of Christ Church College, and I have my own high seat in the chancel, as an Honorary Student.' However, writing in his autobiography (*Works* XXXV: 190) of his undergraduate days at Christ Church between 1937 and 1841, Ruskin recalled 'Even the first sight of college chapel disappointed me, after the large churches abroad. . . . The cathedral itself was an epitome of English history. Every stone, every pane of glass, every panel of woodwork, was true, and of its time, – not an accursed sham of architect's job. . . . The Norman vaults above were true English Norman; bad and rude enough, but the best we could do with our own wits, and no French help. The roof was true Tudor, – grotesque, inventively constructive, delicately carved; . . . The west window, with its clumsy painting of the Adoration of the Shepherds . . . the best man could do of the day; . . .' From the present account, the Ruskins did not appear impressed by their 1830 visit to Christ Church.

6. New College, founded in 1379 by William of Wykeham, lies diagonally across the city from Christ Church. Queen's College would have been between their inn and New College.

The five pieces of sculpture which the Ruskins saw were medieval panels of the Crowning of the Madonna, the Annunciation, Ascension, Nativity and Resurrection. They are now much worn and have been removed from the chapel and placed in the fifteenth century Music Room to the north of the Chapel. They were replaced by the present reredos by Westmacott.

New College Chapel is rich in old glass, boasting the finest fourteenth century windows in Oxford. The windows depicting saints or martyrs which they saw were probably the fourteenth century windows of the ante-chapel behind the screen. The large west window was designed by Sir Joshua Reynolds and made by Thomas Jervais.

Ruskin was later to refer to this Reynolds window on several occasions. In *Sir Joshua and Holbein* (*Works* XIX:7) he says that Reynolds' 'Faiths, Charities, or other well-ordered and emblem-fitted virtues, are even less lovely than his ordinary portraits of women'. In *The Two Paths*

(*Works* XVI:324) he wrote 'No man who knows what painting means, can endure a painted glass window which emulates a painters' work', and in Appendix II to *The Two Paths* (*Works* XVI:417) he explains how Reynolds himself was disappointed with the effect of the windows.

7.   The Sheldonian Theatre, built in 1667 by Sir Christopher Wren for Gilbert Sheldon, Warden of All Souls. The design was based on the Theatre of Marcellus in Rome. The purpose of the building was to house the University Press and to provide the university with a meeting place. It was here on his birthday, 8 February 1870, that Ruskin delivered his inaugural lecture as Slade Professor of Fine Art.

8.   Built between 1737 and 1749 by James Gibbs, the Radcliffe Camera is the largest and most imposing 18th century library in England. Named after Dr John Radcliffe, it was originally intended as a medical library. Since 1860 it has been an extension of the Bodleian. It is adorned by casts of classical statuary.

9.   Magdalene College was founded by William of Wainflete in 1458. The college buildings, built round four quadrangles, occupy some twelve acres. Joseph Addison, whose rooms the Ruskins saw, was one of the authors whose works John James Ruskin used to read aloud to the family. He was a Fellow of Magdalene from 1698 to 1711. The noble chapel was built in the last quarter of the fifteenth century. The great west window with its representation of the Last Judgement, was painted by Christopher Schwarz about 1600 and was restored after gale damage in the eighteenth century. The library, on the west side of the medieval Great Quadrangle, contains part of the Founder's Library. The painting attributed in 1830 to Morelles now forms the altar piece in the college chapel. After Ruskin's time it was attributed to Ribalta but about 1932 T. S. R. Boase discovered evidence which made him reattribute it to Valdès Leal.

The 'curious stone pulpit' is in an angle of St John's Quad, so called after the Hospital of St John on the site which was suppressed by Bishop Wainflete when he founded the college. A sermon is still preached from the pulpit annually on St John's Day.

10.   It is interesting to read Ruskin's reaction – or lack of reaction – to the Hall at Christ Church, which is probably the finest in England after Westminster Hall and where he himself was to dine as a gentleman commoner between 1837 and 1841. He wrote of it in *Praeterita* (*Works* XXXV: 192–4) 'The influence on me of . . . the hall, was of a different and curiously mixed character. Had it only been used . . . for the refectory daily, the reception of guests, the delivery of speeches on state occasions, and the like – the hall, like the cathedral, would have had an entirely salutary and beneficiently solemnizing effect on me. But . . . [Dr] Abbot allowed our hall to be used for "collections" [termly college examinations]. As time went on, the aspect of my college hall to me meant little more than the fear and shame of those examination days; but even in the first surprise and sublimity of finding myself dining there were many reasons for the qualification of my pleasure. The change from our front parlour at Herne Hill, some fifteen feet by eighteen, and meat and pudding with my mother and Mary, to a hall about as big as the nave of Canterbury Cathedral, with its extremity lost in mist, its roof in darkness . . . was in itself more appalling to me than appetizing . . .' There are now over three

hundred portraits in the Christ Church collection, many of the finest
being in the hall. The portrait of the founder of the college, was probably
that by Sampson Strong, 1610–11, while that of Henry VIII was probably
the seventeenth century pastiche attributed to John Taylor, c.1670, which
was derived ultimately from the full-length portrait by Holbein. Richard
Busby (1606–95) was at Christ Church in 1624. From 1638 until his death
he was Headmaster of Westminster School. His anonymous portrait with
a pupil is still in the hall, as indeed are those of Henry VIII and Wolsey.
The portrait of George Canning (1770–1827) is by Lawrence. Canning
was at Christ Church from 1788–91; his third son, Charles John Canning,
later Earl Canning, Governor General of India, was an undergraduate at
Christ Church in 1830.

11.   Blenheim Palace was planned for the Duke of Marlborough by Van-
burgh. The grounds were laid out by Capability Brown who is said to
have planned avenues of trees to represent a plan of the Battle of
Blenheim. At the time of the Ruskins' visits Blenheim was the home of
Spencer George Churchill, 5th Duke of Marlborough (1766–1840). Most
of the paintings seen by Ruskin have now been sold. However the
painting by Reynolds of the fourth Duke and Duchess and their six
children may still be seen in the Red Drawing Room. The painting by
Carlo Dolci of the Adoration of the Magi is still at Blenheim and
Rysbrack's fine statue of Queen Anne is still in the Long Library.

12.   Woodstock Church was originally built in the twelth century as a Chapel
of Ease to neighbouring Bladon Church. Of the original building little
remains and it has been much altered over the years, particularly in the
seventeenth century. The tower is eighteenth century. In the early
nineteenth century there was little interest in the church and for a time it
was closed, the rector only holding services at Bladon. In 1830 the rector
was William Mavor LL.D. (1759–1837). He was a compiler of educational
works and is chiefly known for his *English Spelling Book*, 1801, and *British
Tourists, or Traveller's Pocket Companion*, 1798–1800. Ruskin described this
latter in *Praeterita* (*Works* XXXV:266), as 'a favourite old book'. Mavor was
schoolmaster at Woodstock and was ordained in 1781. In 1810 he became
rector of Bladon-with-Woodstock, a living which he retained for the
remainder of his life. He was a popular man and was mayor of Woodstock
ten times. There is a memorial to Mavor outside the church, between the
porch and the bell tower.

13.   The route from Woodstock would probably have taken them through
Chipping Norton, Moreton-in-Marsh, Broadway, Evesham and Pershore
to Worcester, a distance of some 50 miles. There is no indication of the
hotel in which they spent the night. Ruskin seems to have been strangely
unimpressed by the splendours of Worcester Cathedral with its many fine
early tombs of interesting historical figures. The crypt there is possibly
the finest and second oldest in the country. Not surprisingly he noted the
wall monument by Roubilliac to Bishop Hough, President of Magdalene
College, Oxford, with the bishop reclining above his sarcophagus amid
scenes of his expulsion from Oxford. The tomb of King John is in the
choir between those of the Saxon bishops, Saints Oswald and Wulfstan.
He died at Newark and was buried here at his own wish. His is the oldest
royal effigy in the country. His tomb was opened in 1797. Prince Arthur,
son of Henry VII, died at Ludlow aged 15, and was buried here. His

chantry comprises six bays of open tracery with small flying butresses supporting the vaulted roof, and is one of the finest examples of Tudor art.

14.   The journey from Worcester to Stratford-on-Avon by way of Alcester is about 25 miles. Shakespeare's tomb is in the parish church at Stratford, marked by a plain stone behind the altar rail. The bust, mentioned here, forms part of the monument on the wall to the left. The half-length figure of Shakespeare was carved by the Southwark mason Gerard Johnston. It was made a few years after Shakespeare's death and is probably an acceptable likeness. Before leaving the church Ruskin signed the Visitors' Book on behalf of himself and Mary:

John Ruskin junior   May 25 1830
Miss Richardson

This Visitors' Book, for the years 1825–33, is now preserved at the Birthplace (ER/24). From the church the Ruskins crossed Stratford to visit the Birthplace. The room where they saw all of the signatures was restored in the 1940s. The signatures were photographed as a record and the walls were then whitewashed over. A few signatures, engraved on the window, are preserved. Among the names at one time to be found on the walls were those of Izaak Walton, Robert Browning, Thomas Carlyle, Edmund Keen, and of course Sir Walter Scott. Whether or not all of these worthies actually visited the Birthplace is, of course, a different matter! After the mulberry tree which Shakespeare is said to have planted at New Place was cut down in 1758 there was a proliferation of mulberry souvenirs available to Stratford visitors. In the opinion of Dr Levi Fox, Director of the Shakespeare Birthplace Trust, to whom we are indebted for this information, the mulberry box that Ruskin saw was probably one of the items carved from the authentic tree and this box remains in the collection of the Birthplace Trust. It is illustrated on p.79 of Dr Fox's *In honour of Shakespeare* (Jarrold, 1972). This time it was Mary's turn to sign the Visitors' Book for both of them:

Miss Richardson   25 May 1830
John Ruskin Junior   25 May 1830

The entry occurs in the Birthplace Visitors' Book (DR 185/5, p.60). We are grateful to Dr Fox for drawing our attention to the fact that Ruskin had previously been at the Birthplace two years earlier and Ruskin and his father had signed the Visitors' Book (DR 185/4, p.351)

John Ruskin
Mr & Mrs Ruskin   London   3 June 1828

15.   Stratford to Leamington via Warwick is a journey of only some 10 miles. They arrived in Leamington on Tuesday 25 May and stayed until Monday 31 May. We do not know where they stayed on this visit, although in August 1841 Ruskin stayed at the Bedford Hotel. The rain clearly kept the party indoors for most of the week. However the outing to Warwick was not the only excursion, for we know from John James's Account Book (Bem MS 28) that on 27 May John was taken to the dentist, at a cost of £4 11s 6d.

16.   The visit to Warwick was on 29 May. Since Scott, one of the Ruskin

family's favourite authors, had called Warwick Castle 'that fairest monument of ancient and chivalrous splendour which yet remains uninjured by time', the visit must have been eagerly anticipated. The towers date from the 14th century. Guy's Tower is 128 feet high; Caesar's 147 feet.

17.   Still preserved in the castle is the Civil War armour which belonged to Lord Brooke who, while a Major General commanding the Warwickshire and Staffordshire Militia, was killed at the seige of Lichfield in 1643. Ruskin, who had forgotten Lord Brooke's name, has left a space in the manuscript. The buff coat which Ruskin saw was destroyed in the fire of 1871. On view now is a replica which goes with the suit of armour. Oliver Cromwell's helmet is still preserved in the Armoury.

18.   Up to 1978 when Lord Brooke sold Warwick Castle to Madame Tussaud's there were three pictures in the private apartments by Salvator Rosa:

> 1 Hermit seated among classical ruins reading a book surrounded by emblems of mortality. (58″ × 38″)
>
> 2 & 3 Wooded landscape with Hermit seated on a rock under a tree (both attributed to School of Rosa)

19.   Although there are still a number of portraits by Van Dyke at Warwick, two of the finer pictures have now been sold. They were:

> Portrait of Ferdinand de Boischostt, Baron Saventheim, in black doublet with red cross, white cuffs and ruff, 1630. (43″ × 36″)
>
> Portrait of a nobleman previously thought to be Gondomar, Spanish Ambassador to King James I, but probably the Principe d'Angri, three quarter length in black cloak with gloved hand resting on sword. (40″ × 33″)

There were also Van Dykes of Strafford, Charles Stuart and St Sebastian.

20.   The 'pair of fine lions by Rubens' still graces the State Dining Room. It is believed to be a sketch for the complete picture which is in the Louvre. It is attributed to Franz Snyders who spent much of his time in Rubens's studio. (46″ × 67″)

21.   The 'Warwick Vase', a huge elaborately sculpted white marble urn of 163 gallons capacity was perhaps made by Lysippus over 2000 years ago. It was found in the bed of the lake at Tivoli. It was bought, in pieces, by Sir William Hamilton, the noted collector. He had it restored and he sold it to his nephew, George Greville, Second Earl of Warwick. Clearly Ruskin had not been paying attention and had confused George, Second Earl, with George III! George Greville brought the vase to Warwick where it was placed in the grounds. In 1783–4 he had the Conservatory built to house it. The Warwick Vase is now in the Burrell Collection at Glasgow.

We are indebted for much of our information on Warwick to Mr F. H. P. Barker, the Curator of the Castle.

22.   We have no indication of where the Ruskins stayed, but Wrightson's *Annual Directory of Birmingham* for 1829 lists the following central hotels; Fountain Inn (Jno. Hart), 136 New Street; Hen & Chickens Inn & Hotel (Wm. Waddell), New Street; Swan (Theodore Wakefield) High Street and New Street; Red Lion (Margaret Welch), 2 Bull Ring.

23.   Wrightson's *Annual Directory* lists Museum (Natural History), 38 New Street.

24. Wrightson's *Annual Directory* lists Thomas Phipson, Pin and Needle Maker, Little Cannon Street; and Thorpe, Lathom & Kilminster, 137 Lancaster Street. Wrightson's *Directory* for 1831 adds Kirby, Beard and Kirby, of Anne Street.

25. Probably the newly built Theatre Royal in New Street. During that week Mr Macready's company was performing there. On Tuesday 1 June the programme included the plays *Venice Preserved* and *The Brigand*, with Mr Macready taking the part of Pierre in *Venice Preserved*. We are indebted to Mr Patrick Baird of the Local Studies Dept., Birmingham Libraries Department for this information.

26. Sir Francis Chantry (1781–1841), sculptor. The monument, one of Lichfield's best known, is to the two daughters of William Robinson who both died by fire in 1812. It has been called the Snowdrop Monument.

27. Ruskin probably refers here to the Herkenrode windows in the Lady Chapel. The glass in these seven tall narrow windows was originally at the Belgian abbey of Herkenrode near Liége. It was taken out of the abbey and stored during the French occupation of Belgium in Napoleon's time. In 1803 it was bought by Sir Brooke Boothby and brought to Lichfield. He is said to have paid £200 for the whole collection, which is among the most beautiful glass in England.

28. Lady Mary Wortley Montague (1689–1762) who introduced the practice of innoculation for smallpox into England in 1718. The monument is a tribute to Lady Montague from a lady saved from smallpox by innoculation.

29. The monument is to the parents and sister of Anna Seward, 'The Swan of Lichfield' (1747–1809) authoress, who lived in the town from 1754. About 1776 she first met Boswell to whom she afterwards communicated information concerning Dr Johnson, with whom she was acquainted. She also included among her acquaintances Erasmus Darwin, Thomas Day, R. L. Edgeworth, Dr Parr, John Howard and Sir Walter Scott to whom she bequeathed her literary works and remains. The lines by Scott conclude with his tribute to Anne Seward:

> Her worth, her warmth of heart, our sorrows say:
> Go, seek her genius in the living lay.

30. Dr Samuel Johnson (1709–1784), lexicographer, was the son of a Lichfield bookseller. He was born at his father's shop in Breadmarket Street, at one corner of the Market Place. At the beginning of the last century the large downstairs room (formerly Michael Johnson's bookshop), was let as a shop, with the shopman living in the rooms above; some of the other rooms may also have been let to lodgers. In March 1826 the premises were occupied by William Evans, tinsmith and brazier. It is clear from contemporary acounts that Evans was quite happy for visitors to see over the house, but whether or not the Ruskins actually entered the house is not clear. The building was opened to the public in 1901 as the Johnson Birthplace Museum.

31. Derby had the first silk-thread mill in England. It was built in 1717 on an island in the Derwent by John Lombe. Later, one of the largest factories for the manufacture of artificial silk was established in the town.

32. Kedleston Hall, the seat of Lord Scarsdale, is about four miles north west of Derby, in the Ashbourne direction. It was built by the Adam Brothers

for the first Lord Scarsdale (c.1761). It is a fine house with a 360 foot frontage. Dr Johnson is reported to have considered it more suitable for a town hall than a house. The entrance hall has a vaulted ceiling supported by twenty corinthian columns. This is probably Ruskin's 'Corinthian hall'. His 'extremely light and elegant' room may have been the domed saloon, 63 feet high and divided into Grecian alcoves.

33. Matlock Bath is one of the several Matlocks which are grouped together on the side of the river Derwent in this part of Derbyshire. Ruskin would perhaps not consider it quite as attractive today. The town began in 1698 when the first bath was built over a warm spring. On one side the valley is bordered by the 1111 feet high hill, Masson, and on the other by High Tor rising sheer to some 4000 feet above the river. The exploitation of Matlock Bath was slow to develop but with the opening to the public of the first mine – the Cumberland Cavern – in about 1800, the boom began, and the beautiful location has subsequently developed into the Spa which we know today. By 1830 when Ruskin visited Matlock nine show caves were open to the public. In the main, these were adapted lead mines.

At Matlock the Ruskins stayed at George Saxton's New Bath Hotel and it was here that Ruskin's interest in mineralogy developed. In *Praeterita* (*Works* XXXV:75) he wrote

> . . . in the glittering white broken spar, speckled with galena, by which the walks of the hotel garden were made bright, and in the shops of the pretty village, and in many a happy walk among its cliffs, I pursued my mineralogical studies on fluor, calcite, and the ores of lead, with indescribable rapture when I was allowed to go into a cave. My father and mother showed far more kindness than I knew, in yielding to my subterranean passion; for my mother could not bear dirty places, and my father had a nervous feeling that the ladders would break, or the roof fall, before we got out again . . .

In *Praeterita* Ruskin inaccurately dates this visit as 1829. However there is no evidence that they visited Derbyshire in that year, and it is evident that his first visit was in 1830. He was there again briefly in 1851 and subsequently wrote to his father from Venice (*Works* IX:xlvii, n) that 'I found our old inland haunt, Matlock, little changed, and very sweet and quiet . . . From the New Bath Hotel in 1867 Ruskin wrote to his mother on 23 August (Bem B VI; *Works* XXXVI:541) '. . . I am at the old Inn, which Mary drew, in the old times. It is added to a little – but what was of it, remains and looks much as it did. The green flat in front – and the tree, are just the same – the garden where I used to play, & gather bits of lead ore, is still there – and the walks still sprinkled with spar . . .' Again, in 1871 Ruskin was staying in (by now Ivatt's) New Bath Hotel when he was taken ill and was nursed by Joan Severn and Mrs Cowper-Temple. The visit of 1871 was probably Ruskin's longest, lasting from 26 June until 30 July. However, the 1830 visit, which was split into two parts, was of similar duration. At this time they arrived on 4 June and stayed definitely until the 7th and possibly the 11th, returning on 19 July and staying until 2 August.

A Matlock Directory for 1829 lists George Saxton as victualler of the New Bath Hotel and the land tax assessment for 1830 shows the Bath Hotel and land owned by the New Bath Company and occupied by Mr

Saxton. Saxton held, in addition to the hotel and grounds, five other pieces of land owned by five different owners, but all described under the heading 'Bath Hotel and land'. If all of these pieces of land were in fact held together as part of the hotel and grounds, the New Bath Hotel must have had the most extensive grounds in the Spa. We are indebted to Miss Sinar of the Derbyshire Records Office for this information.

34. High Tor, on the left bank of the river, rises to a height of some 350 feet. Glover's *Peak Guide*, (1830), tells us that the 'lower part is covered with small trees and underwood, of various foliage; but the upper part, for fifty or sixty yards, is one broad mass of naked perpendicular rocks'.

35. About 1825 the west end of Coalpit Rake was opened to the public as The Devonshire Cavern, in honour of the Duke of Devonshire. The Cavern, which comprises openings into immense natural cavities, lies under the Heights of Abraham, the name given to the top part of Masson Hill, immediately across the river from High Tor.

36. Willersley Castle at Cromford, a short distance from Matlock, was built by Sir Richard Arkwright (1732–92) in 1788 from plans by William Thomas. Arkwright, a pioneer of the cotton spinning industry, is buried at Cromford Church. His son, Richard Arkwright (1755–1843), who amassed a large fortune as a mill-owner, lived at Willersley Castle in 1830. His gardens and pleasure grounds extended to eight acres and here, for the seven years before Ruskin's visit, he had planted annually 50 000 trees. He won a number of medals from the Society of Arts for producing grapes in the winter. Willersley Castle is now a Methodist Guild Holiday and Conference Centre.

37. It is predictable that the Ruskins would buy mementoes of the places they visited, because that was what was expected of the tourist. 'Partly in my father's sense of what was kind and proper to be done, – partly by way of buying "a trifle from Matlock" . . .', wrote Ruskin in *Praeterita* (*Works* XXXV:267) of their purchases in Rome in 1840–41. John James's accounts (Bem MS 28) record the 1830 purchases as 'Spar Bull and Cow 56/-, Vase 30/-, Bath £3 10s, Adrian Vase 21/-, small do. and [?] carriage 25/-'. In the Journal Ruskin had originally written '. . . also a Roman sarcophagus costing 50 shillings in black . . .' Subsequently he changed 'sarcophagus' to 'bath' and deleted the inaccurate 50 shillings.

38. The Dog and Partridge (Pigot's *Commercial Directory for Derbyshire*, 1835, shows the landlord as James Yates) is about a mile from the village of Thorpe, and about 14 miles south west of Matlock, to the west of the Ashbourne–Buxton road.

39. Strictly speaking, Dovedale is not a dale, but a narrow gorge-like valley some three miles in length. The cone-shaped hill, Thorpe Cloud, is 942 feet in height, on the Derbyshire side of the river, while on the Staffordshire side, Bunster rises to 1000 feet.

40. The features which Ruskin mentions are all well-known landmarks. The Sugarloaves, or Tissington Spires, form a group of jagged rock pinnacles similar in appearance to the famous needle rocks at Cheddar. Dovedale Church is the name given to a deeply fissured mass of rock. In front of Reynard's Cave is a large natural arch perforating a ridge of rock only a few feet wide. The approach to Reynard's Cave is still very steep and covered by small, loose stones, but one of the main hazards today is the number of people ascending and descending the slope!

41. Haddon Hall is situated near the Buxton–Matlock road, between Bake-well and Rowsley. It is one of the most attractive of the ancient manor houses of the country, parts of the building being Norman or possibly Saxon in origin. The house was added to between 1300 and 1380. Further additions were made up to about 1530. The house passed from the Vernon family to the Dukes of Portland with the marriage of Dorothy Vernon and John Manners in Tudor times. The house still belongs to the Duke of Portland. It was uninhabited throughout the eighteenth and nineteenth centuries and thoroughly restored after 1912 by the ninth duke. The house evidently impressed Ruskin and he wrote his poem *Haddon Hall* which is printed in the Appendix. He returned in 1837 to make drawings of the house. The early painted glass, which Ruskin mentions as once having been in the chapel, had in fact been stolen two years before his visit. The extensive wall paintings there had not been uncovered in Ruskin's time. His 'rotten tapestry' may be the tapestries representing hunting scenes made in Brussels about 1500 which are now in the State Bedroom. The tapestries have long been among the principal features of Haddon. They remained there when the house was almost unfurnished and have survived many years of neglect although about sixty pieces were destroyed in a fire in 1925. Much of the furniture and other objects which Ruskin saw are still in the house. 'The bust of an aunt of the Duke of Portland's' is constructed from the death mask of Lady Grace Manners, daughter-in-law of Dorothy Vernon.

42. Chatsworth, about three miles from Haddon Hall, was bought in the sixteenth century by Sir William Cavendish and it has been the principal country seat of the Cavendish family since that time. The present house was built by the first Duke of Devonshire, work beginning in 1687. William Talman designed the south and east fronts and Thomas Archer was probably responsible for the north front. The greatest artists of the day were employed for the carving, sculpting and painting. Considerable extensions were made to the house by the sixth duke between 1820 and 1827. These were designed by Sir Jeffry Wyatville and include the modern Dining Room, Sculpture Gallery, Orangery and Theatre. The Library took on its present appearance about 1830 and the sixth duke bought two complete libraries to add to the books already in the house. When the Ruskins visited Chatsworth it was still the home of William Spencer Cavendish, sixth Duke of Devonshire.

The house and gardens were open to any interested visitors from the time they were built and laid out by the first duke. Chatsworth became generally more accessible with the improvement of the roads in the late eighteenth century when a special inn for travellers was built at Edensor, on the estate. The number of visitors increased throughout the nine-teenth century, partly attracted by the great additions made by the sixth duke. A visitors' Book survives from this period and we are indebted to the Librarian at Chatsworth, Mr P. J. Day, for drawing our attention to the entry for 11 June 1830 which reads 'Mr Ruskin and family'. The 'Seven Wonders of Derbyshire' include Chatsworth and Mam Tor and Peak Cavern at Castleton, all of which Ruskin was to see during the course of the tour.

The Ruskins must have breakfasted late, after seeing Haddon Hall, perhaps at the Edensor Inn, near Chatsworth, where the landlord was a

Mr Walters.

43. Most of the works of art mentioned by Ruskin in his account of Chatsworth are still in the house, and again we are indebted to Mr Day for identifying them. Ruskin's 'beautiful gilt vase with a smaller one' probably referred to the gilt lead vases by the sculptor Cibber, now in the North sub-corridor. The statue of Mars and Cupid is a marble group by Gibson now in the Sculpture Gallery. There are a number of antique busts now in the Painted Hall although there is no reference to their having come from Herculaneum, and even Ruskin was unsure of this because the reference to that town has been crossed out in the manuscript. The marble bust of Alexander is now to be seen in the north Entrance Hall. The Old Master drawings are now all stored in cases, but when Ruskin visited Chatsworth, many were on display in the Sketch Galleries on the top floor. Mr Day is unable to identify the 'two large Indian chests', but the red Porphyry Vases and the statue of Hebe by Canova are both now in the Sculpture Gallery. There too are the marble tables with gryphon (not vulture) supports, the statues of Endymion by Canova and Ganymede by Tadolini. There is a malachite table in the Sculpture Gallery and another in the State Rooms. Canova's bust of Napoleon and the statue of Madame Bonaparte are both in the Sculpture Gallery, while Westmacott's statue of Mary, Queen of Scots, was later removed by the sixth duke to Hardwick Hall, another Devonshire house, where it remains on the Garden Terrace.

44. The gardens and grounds are one of the glories of Chatsworth. They were originally laid out in the formal French style for the first duke and were later re-modelled in the landscape style in the eighteenth century by the fourth duke. The gardens, as they are seen today, are mainly the creation of the sixth duke (1790–1858). His gardener was (Sir) Joseph Paxton and his architect Sir Jeffry Wyatville. Many features of the earlier gardens survive today, but the gardens which the present visitor sees had not been created in 1830. 'The waterworks' which so impressed Ruskin, still survive, and are operated by water under natural pressure which comes from a series of mainly man-made lakes above the house to the east. The Cascade Temple, at the top of Ruskin's 'steep hill', was built in 1703 probably from a design by the Birmingham architect Thomas Archer. The water, which comes from all of its fountains, then runs for 200 yards down a wide flight of steps, falling 60 feet. This impressive watercourse survives from the first duke's garden, and was designed for him by Grillet. Having run its course, the water disappears at the foot of the steps, to re-appear in the Sea-horse Fountain. The Copper or Willow Tree Fountain is the successor to another relic of the first duke's garden. The original tree was cast in 1692 and was re-cast or replaced in the early nineteenth century by the present tree. It is a very realistic copper willow tree in a wooded part of the garden. Water plays from the branches of the tree and the little clearing in which it is located is surrounded by powerful jets. The 'large sheet of water' is the 250 yards long Canal Pond, dug for the first duke in 1703. It served the dual purpose of being decorative, and also supplying ice to stock the now disused ice house. The Emperor Fountain, with its 290 feet high jet was installed in the Canal Pond for the sixth duke by Paxton and was first used in July 1844. This must have replaced the earlier and shorter jet which Ruskin saw. Between Canal

Pond and the south front of the house is the Sea-horse Fountain, another survivor of the first duke's formal garden of the 1690s. The sea-horses were carved by Cibber.

45. From Chatsworth to Buxton is a distance of some 13 miles. The last few miles of the journey pass through Wye Dale and Ashwood Dale. Ashwood Dale is a rocky-sided valley, in parts bare and sombre, in other parts wooded or clad with ferns and evergreens.

46. Buxton had long been known as a spa and had a number of springs which were said to possess medical properties. Eventually its popularity outgrew its facilities and between 1780 and 1796 the fifth Duke of Devonshire built The Crescent, The Square and The Great Stables. These provided Assembly Rooms, hotels, boarding and private houses. The architect was John Carr (1723–1807). The church of St John the Baptist was also built by the duke and would have been relatively new at the time of the Ruskins' visit. The minister in 1830 was George Trevor Spencer who was here from 1824 until 1838. There were many hotels in the town at the time of the Ruskins' visit and we have no indication of which one they used.

47. The route from Buxton would have taken them north–west through Whaley Bridge, Disley and Stockport, into Manchester, a distance of about 20 miles.

48. Manchester was by this time a substantial manufacturing city. Again we have no indication of where the Ruskins stayed. An average of statistics taken between 1807 and 1824 show that June, in fact, was one of the driest months in Manchester, with only 12 wet days and 2.433 inches of rain.

49. The route from Manchester to Liverpool is by way of Warrington and is a distance of 37 miles.

50. John James Ruskin, who often had to visit Liverpool in connection with his business, stayed at the Adelphi Hotel, built at the end of Ranelagh Street in 1826. It was the principal hotel of the town although it was often criticized by JJR. On 31 December 1836 he wrote, to his wife, 'I detest this Adelphi – all comfortless – Splendid misery.' (Bem L 2, published by Burd, op. cit., p.401). It is evident from Ruskin's letter to his father of 21 February 1829 (Yale Vol 1, published by Burd, op. cit. p.177) that he himself had also stayed at the Adelphi before the visit of 1830. Presumably the family had found it necessary to visit Liverpool *en route* for Scotland in either 1824 or 1826 and the young Ruskin had remembered their rooms. 'When I heard you were at the Adelphi I had the small crimson glass windowed room, the other larger room the Adelphi itself, the street down which our window looked, the Mersey &c all before my eyes at the same instant.' From the Adelphi to the river would be a distance of about three quarters of a mile.

51. We have been unable to identify the ship which sailed for New York. This poem, while being the only one which Ruskin included in the Journal, is by no means the only one which he composed during the journey. He began writing *The Day of Judgement* (see Appendix) on 22 May and finished it on 13 June, just two days before the arrival in Liverpool. *Haddon Hall* was also written in June or July.

52. The first public railway to use steam locomotives, the Stockton and Darlington Railway, was opened on 27 September 1825. By this time

plans were already advanced for the building of the Liverpool to Manchester Railway. The enabling Act of Parliament was passed in 1826 and work began immediately. The 12 square miles of marshy Chat Moss had to be drained, the Olive Mount Cutting, nearly 2 miles in length and in places 80 feet deep was the first stone cutting of considerable size ever made for a railway. 63 bridges had to be built to carry the railway, and a 2000 yards long tunnel under Liverpool had to be cut. Up to 1829 some of the directors favoured the idea of the motive power being supplied by stationary engines and haulage ropes. However, the Rainhill Trials, in October 1829, which were won by Stephenson's *Rocket*, convinced the directors that steam locomotion should be used on the line. Eventually work was completed between Crown Street Station in Liverpool and Liverpool Road Station in Manchester and the first passenger train ran on 15 September 1830, conveying the Duke of Wellington, Sir Robert Peel, and others, from Liverpool to Manchester, a timetabled journey of two hours for the 31 miles. Work on the railway would have been nearing completion in June 1830 when Ruskin saw the railway. On 8 March in the following year JJR was in Liverpool again, and he saw the railway operating. His account, in a letter to his son, is printed in the Appendix.

53. The foundation stone for the St James's Cemetery, situated at the top of Duke Street to the south of the city, was laid on 28 August 1827. Most of the stone for the building of the city came from this quarry, which comprises some 44000 square yards. It was clearly one of the 'sites' of Liverpool; the chapel was described as 'a beautiful specimen of classical architecture . . . it has the appearance of a temple, the portico is formed of six Doric columns supporting an entablature and pediment . . .' (G. N. Wright & T. Allen: *Lancashire*, n.d., II, 171) William Huskisson, killed at the opening of the Liverpool and Manchester Railway, was buried in this cemetery.

54. Edward Baines: *History, Directory and Gazetteer of the County Palatine of Lancaster*, (1824), explains that there were several Mersey crossing points, but at this time the mail was carried across the river on the Liverpool–Woodside ferry. The steamers operating this route in 1830 were the paddle steamers Royal Mail, Frances, Hercules, St David and King Fisher. The only steamer called St George which was regularly plying from Liverpool at this time was the one operated by the St George Steam Packet Company. This St George was powered by a 100 h.p. engine and sailed from Liverpool to Dublin every Monday, Wednesday and Friday, taking 12 hours for the passage. She alternated on the route with the Emerald Isle (150 h.p.) who sailed on Tuesdays, Thursdays and Saturdays. Clearly something had gone amiss with the timetable at this time, because on Thursday 17 June one would have expected Ruskin to see the Emerald Isle arrive, in readiness to sail later in the day.

55. From Liverpool to Preston is 32 miles. At Preston they stayed at Thomas Prescott's Black Bull in Friargate, as is evident from the account of the return visit. On Sunday they possibly attended St George's Chapel (built in 1723) situated between Fishergate and Friargate, which was one of the several churches and chapels in Preston. (Baines: *Directory* II, 486)

56. Garstang is exactly mid-way between Preston and Lancaster, 11 miles from each. The posting houses there were James M'Kee's Royal Oak in the Market Place, and Ellen Walker's Eagle and Child in the High Street.

Public accommodation at the inns was described as 'good'. (Baines, op. cit.) The inhabitants of Garstang were said to be long-lived and in 1830 there were 25 persons whose cumulative age was 2000 years. The ruins of Greenhalgh Castle, a short distance from the town, was built in the reign of Henry VII. In 1645 the castle belonged to Lord Derby and was dismantled in 1649 by order of Parliament.

57.   Lancaster stands on the estuary of the river Lune and from the higher parts of the city the Lake District hills can be seen across Morecambe Bay. Lancaster Castle was originally built in the eleventh century and at the time of the Ruskins' visit it housed the court, administrative offices and prisons. The foundations of a new tower were laid in July 1818; it was completed in May 1821 and was used to house female prisoners. An average of 150 debtors and 185 criminals were usually housed in the castle at this time. In 1824 Baines (op. cit. II, 16) wrote 'A terrace on the south side of the castle, and another on the north, communicate by the west, and form a fine promenade, where the gay are refreshed by the pure air and delighted with the beauties of the surrounding scenery.' The Ruskins put up at the King's Arms in Market Street, near the castle, where John Pritt was landlord.

58.   Kendal, in Westmorland, is 21 miles from Lancaster, situated then on the main road north, and being one of the principal towns on the edge of the Lake District, Kendal was always busy and was well furnished with coaching inns with their yards at the side and an arch giving access on to the main street. We are unsure where the Ruskins stayed but it was probably at John Jackson's King's Arms in Stricklandgate which was demolished in 1934. Another posting house listed in Parsons & White's *Directory of Cumberland and Westmorland* (1829), where they may have stayed was the Commercial in Highgate, where the innkeeper was James Webster.

59.   Their route lay along the main road from Kendal to Windermere and thence along the side of the lake to Low Wood, a distance of 12 miles. For many years the Low Wood had been one of the district's principal hotels and it had been 'improved' a few years before the visit. T. Robinson's advertisement for the hotel in the *Westmorland Advertiser* of 28 May 1825 indicated that the inn was 'now fitted up in the first style of elegance, having had new stables erected equal to any in the kingdom, with every other corresponding accommodation which can be found in the first houses on the road.' Writing in retrospect, Ruskin described Low Wood in *Praeterita* as 'little more than a country cottage'. He was to stay here again in 1837 and 1838. In 1867 he found the hotel much changed – '. . . too noisy and fashionable – Manchester fashion . . .' he wrote to his mother. (JR–MR, 30 June 1867, *Bem* B VI)

60.   Ambleside, a mile and a half along the road from the Low Wood Inn, was a small market town, and already a tourists' resort with two hotels, the White Lion and the Saluation, in addition to a number of boarding houses. By 1867 the road along the side of the lake had been 'improved' and Ruskin told his mother, (8 August 1867, *Bem* B VI) 'I have been walking on the old road between Low Wood and Ambleside. On the old *ground*, I should have said, for the old *road* is no more. Widened, walled, levelled, deformed – desolated with fineries and town conveniences – and very profoundly woeful to my eyes.' Ruskin was at fault in describing the

Langdale Pikes as being 'to the right'. He would have seen them in fact, to his left, about 6 miles away, with Scafell beyond them, 11 miles from the Low Wood–Ambleside road.

61. Stock Ghyll Force, in the grounds of James Ladyman's Saluation Hotel, is one of the Lake District's much-admired waterfalls. The water falls about 70 feet.

62. From 1813 until his death in 1850 William Wordsworth lived at Rydal Mount, a little over a mile north of Ambleside.

63. Grasmere is a small town six miles north of Low Wood. The inns at Grasmere in 1830 were the Swan on the main road, and the Red Lion in the village. In *Iteriad* I, 305–6, Ruskin wrote

> At the inn which is built on the bank of the lake
> We determined our luncheon or dinner to take.

There is in fact *no* inn on the edge of the lake, but Jonathan Bell's Red Lion in the village is probably where they stopped.

64. Butterlip How, two or three hundred yards from the centre of the village.

65. As the coach left Grasmere and climbed Dunmail Raise, the beginnings of Helveyn are on the right, with Helm Crag on the left. In fact Helveyn is 3118 feet high.

66. At Legburthwaite, at the head of Thirlmere, they forked right, off the main Keswick road through St John's in the Vale. This is an easier though slightly longer route. Much of Scott's poem *The Bride of Triermain* is set in St John's in the Vale and this may have accounted for the detour. A little farther along, they stopped to admire the Bronze Age stone circle of Castlerigg, which is mentioned in *Iteriad* I, 467.

67. In *Iteriad* I, 481–2, Ruskin wrote

> And now we arrived at the brow of the hill
> Where the vast vale of Keswick lay sweetly and still.

On 9 July 1867 Ruskin wrote to his mother (*Bem* B VI; Dearden: *Iteriad*, p.48) 'The descent on the vale of Keswick by the hill – some mile and a half long, of the old mail road, is supremely beautiful, and people were better taking 4 days to reach the lakes, and so approaching them, than now coming from London in nine hours [by train] and being projected very nearly into the lake out of a tunnel.'

68. Skiddaw is 3054 feet high. Derwentwater is 3 miles in length and 1 mile wide. There are three islands, and from time to time various 'floating islands' have appeared. Saddleback, or Blencathra as it is more correctly known, is 2847 feet high.

69. The drive from Low Wood had been 20 miles. Parsons & White (op. cit. 326) describe Keswick as 'a small but neat market town, consisting of one long street of good houses'. There were inns, many lodging houses, two museums, a town hall and a savings bank. The Ruskins put up at the Royal Oak Hotel, innkeeper Joseph Hudson. The Royal Oak is one of the oldest hotels in Keswick and at that time was the chief posting and coaching inn. Among its well-known patrons were Scott, Tennyson, Stevenson and Wordsworth. The Southeys, Coleridge and John Peel were frequent visitors. Ruskin had almost certainly stayed here in 1824 and 1826 *en route* for Scotland and he later wrote (probably of the 1824 visit) 'The first thing which I remember as an event in life was being taken by

my nurse to the brow of Friars Crag on Derwentwater'. (*Modern Painters* III, ch.xvii, para 13; *Works* V:365) The Ruskin Memorial on Friars Crag is engraved with this quotation and was unveiled in 1901. In 1848 Ruskin spent twelve days of his honeymoon here though in 1867 he found the Royal Oak 'only a commercial inn' and he moved on to Bassenthwaite. The hotel is now part of the Trust House group; it has a room named after Ruskin and a stained glass window in his honour.

70. In fact Castle Head, a well-known local vantage point immediately to the south of the town. Jonathan Otley in his *Concise Description of the English Lakes*, (Keswick 1830), describes it as 'a wooded rock rising to 280 feet above the lake'.

71. Crosthwaite's Museum was situated in the Market Place just a few yards from the Royal Oak, 'a little below the middle of Keswick'. According to Crosthwaite's 1792 handbill, 'His house is the loftiest in *Keswick*, and has the Advantage of most delightful Prospects quite round the Vale.' It was not situated in the Town Hall, but in the middle of the Market Place, as mentioned by Cook & Wedderburn. (*Works* II: 296n.) Peter Crosthwaite was born in Cumberland in 1735; after serving with the East India Company for many years he finally settled in Keswick and made a successful living by catering for the 'needs' of tourists. He produced a series of maps of the Lake District, and an improved version of the aeolian harp which was manufactured and sold extensively throughout Cumberland and Westmorland in the eighteenth and nineteenth centuries. The handbill advertising his museum (admittance to Ladies and Gentlemen one shilling each; country People, Sixpence each) says that its contents 'consist of many Hundred Natural and Artificial Curiosities, from every Quarter of the World', many of which no doubt he collected during his time with the East India Co. He died on 9 June 1808 and the running of the museum was continued by his son Daniel. It was eventually closed in 1870.

72. In its present form the aeolian harp seems to have existed since the sixteenth–seventeenth centuries. It consists of a number of gut strings of different thicknesses tuned in unison and stretched on a wooden resonance box. The harp was then usually fitted along the outside of a windowsill. The wind, blowing on the strings, produced a sound similar to that often heard from telegraph wires, but with the added resonance produced by the sound box.

73. William Gell, who visited the museum in 1797 described 'a chinese Gong which produced a most thundering sound. [Crosthwaite] has mirrors in every direction at the windows, by which he instantly sees every carriage that comes from any of the neighbouring towns, though he sits not near any of the windows himself . . . the old woman runs upstairs and rattles away at the Gong, in a manner that cannot fail to attract the notice of the unfortunate strangers in the street. He has even attempted to make a larger Gong, than that he has already, with which he might astonish strangers . . .' (William Gell: *Tour of the Lakes*, Newcastle, 1968, pp.13–14)

74. Plumbago, or graphite, was mined extensively in Borrowdale and used for the manufacture of Black Lead for stoves and grate polish, and in the manufacture of pencils.

75. Crosthwaite discovered the musical properties of stones in 1785 and collected stones to make up two octaves. The playing of musical stones

became very popular in the early nineteenth century. The three Cumberland brothers Richardson performed on them for a season in London before touring America for a year. Their gigantic five octave instrument is now in the Keswick Museum. In 1829 sets of tuned limestones were being offered for sale at William Todhunter's museum in Kendal and they were probably also available elsewhere in the Lake District. The instrument was known variously as a stone dulcimer, a rock harmonicon or a geological piano. Ruskin had one made from Skiddaw slate by Mr Till of Keswick, probably in the 1880s. It used to stand outside the front door at Brantwood and is now in the Coniston Museum. There is an account of this subject in the *Transactions of the Cumberland Association for the Advancement of Literature and Science*, part III, 1877–8, p.155.

76. Crosthwaite Church is less than a mile north of Keswick. The vicar from 1820 until 1855 was the Revd James Lynn. It seems more than probable that the vicar's eight-year-old daughter Elizabeth was in church on that day. She was to grow up to become the popular Victorian novelist Eliza Lynn Linton. The Linton was added to her name when she married W. J. Linton, the author and wood engraver, in 1858, and went to live at Brantwood, Coniston. By coincidence, Ruskin was to buy Brantwood from Linton in 1871.

77. Robert Southey (1774–1843), poet and man of letters, Poet Laureate, lived at Greta Hall, near Keswick, between 1803 and 1843. According to Canon Rawnsley, a later incumbent of Crosthwaite, Southey sat 'in a square pew gay with blue paint, on the south side of the chancel near the pulpit'. (F. C. Eeles: *The Paris Church of St Kentigern, Crosthwaite*, (1953), p.72)

In *Iteriad*, Ruskin wrote:

Next morning the church, how we wished for the reaching!
I'm afraid 'twas as much for the poet as preaching!
. . .
His hair was no colour at all by the way,
But half of't was black, slightly scattered with grey;
His eyes were black as a coal, but in turning
They flashed, – ay, as much as that coal does in burning!
His nose in the midst took a small outward bend,
Rather hooked like an eagle's, and sharp at the end;
But his dark lightening-eye made him seem half-inspired
Or like his own Thalaba, vengefully fired.

78. The Ruskins' heavy travelling carriage would have been quite unsuitable for the 23 mile excursion on which they were about to embark and they would have hired their open carriage and ponies, probably at the Royal Oak. We know from *Iteriad* that they also engaged the services of a guide.

79. Lodore is one of the highest waterfalls in the area, but in dry weather it sometimes fails. One compensation for the rainy weather would be that the Ruskins would see Lodore at its best.

80. Castle Crag, one mile south of Grange-in-Borrowdale, was Thomas West's fourth station and he extols the merits of the view from there in his *Guide to the Lakes*. Although he refers to the remains of a Roman station on the summit, more recent research suggests this is extremely doubtful, despite the Roman pottery and red sandstone found there.

81. West (op. cit.) says of the Bowder Stone, 'This loose stone is of prodigious
     bulk. It lies like a ship on its keel – its length is 62 feet; its circumference
     84. Its solidity is about 23090 feet and its weight about 1771 tons.'
     Clarke's *Survey of the Lakes*, (1789), gives different measurements, but
     since West's measurements are almost exactly repeated by Ruskin,
     perhaps they were using his *Guide*; certainly Ruskin later owned a copy of
     the book. In Ruskin's day the road went round the stone though it has
     now been by-passed and cannot be seen from the present road. It belongs
     to the National Trust.

82. The road from Seatoller over Honister Pass to Buttermere was at that
     time unsuitable for vehicular traffic. The carriage would have returned to
     Keswick and then later driven out by the less precipitous road through
     the Vale of Newlands to Buttermere. Meanwhile Margaret Ruskin and
     Mary Richardson mounted the two ponies which had been brought for
     the purpose and rode the remaining five miles over Honister Pass and
     past Buttermere Lake, accompanied by John, his father and the guide, on
     foot.

83. Gatesgarthdale Beck, which runs from the top of Honister Pass into
     Buttermere, follows the road for most of the way, twice crossing it.

84. Buttermere is one of the smaller lakes, only a mile in length. About a mile
     of land separates it from the next lake, Crummock Water, which is 2½
     miles long.

85. The Fish Inn, at Buttermere, landlord as shown by Parsons and White
     (op. cit.) Jonathan Payle, is situated roughly midway between Buttermere
     and Crummock Water, at the junction of the road which had brought the
     Ruskins over Honister Pass, with the alternative route to Keswick. The
     route which they had followed had brought them 14 miles from Keswick,
     and they had walked or ridden the last 5½ miles, the 2½ miles to the top
     of Honister at an average gradient of 1:4.

     Up to a few years before the Ruskins' visit, the Fish Inn had been
     kept by Mr Robinson, the father of Mary, known as 'The Beauty of
     Buttermere'. Her charm and good looks had been much extolled in guide
     books of the period and most tourists made a pilgrimage to the Fish to see
     her. In 1802 she was married to John Hatfield, the forger and bigamist.
     He had posed as 'The Hon. Colonel Hope', and was hanged at Carlisle in
     the following year. Mary Robinson's story became the subject of many
     poems, stories and even a melodrama.

86. In *Iteriad* Ruskin devotes fourteen lines to the wares which were exhibited
     and of which he did not have a very high opinion!

87. His opinion of the Fish wasn't enhanced when dinner came either! In
     Iteriad he reported

          But there was no treat for the good-dinner lovers.
          Though our appetites were most tremendously high
          We only got taties and mouldy veal pie!

88. They left the Fish Inn in a thunder storm accompanied by heavy rain.
     The ladies began the return journey on foot because one of them was
     afraid to ride up the very steep hill outside the inn in the carriage which
     had returned from Keswick to meet them. The return journey, through
     the Vale of Newlands, was one of 9 miles.

89. In *Iteriad* Ruskin wrote

Cakes, sandwiches, ham, were by no means unhandy;
And amongst other things we forgot not some brandy.

Mountaineering at the end of the eighteenth and beginning of the
nineteenth century was considered a tremendous adventure and not one
which was to be undertaken lightly or without adequate provision. Otley
(*A Concise Description of the English Lakes and adjacent Mountains*, (5th edn,
1833, p.54), in describing the ascent of Skiddaw, says, 'In a small hollow,
if the weather is not too droughty, we meet with a spring of water; and as
it is the last by the way, it may be taken advantage of to dilute the brandy,
which – with a few biscuits or sandwiches – a provident guide will not fail
to recommend.' No doubt the Ruskins had procured the best guide and
had taken his advice. Thirty seven years later Ruskin wrote to tell his
mother that he had been up Skiddaw again (*Bem* B VI, 6 August 1867),
and that on the return trip 'I met a strong looking man in a guide's charge
– panting for breath – He asked me if I had such a thing as a drop of
brandy, for he had forgotten to bring any up. I told him, "it was not the
least cold on the top & he could rest there as long as he liked – and he
would be much better off with no brandy".'

90.   The first part of the route to Skiddaw at that time lay out of Keswick by
the side of the river along the Penrith road for half a mile. At the point
where the road crossed the river, one turned right by Greta Bank. Here,
turning acutely to the left, the track skirted Lattrigg.

91.   Probably Whit Beck, and probably the place where Otley recommended
the drinking of the brandy.

92.   The highest point of Skiddaw which can be seen from Keswick is the
southern end of the ridge which is covered by fragments of slaty rock.
The summit is at the further end of the ridge. Here, Otley records, is a
'large pile of stones, with a central staff 30 feet high, erected in 1826 by a
detachment of the ordnance surveyors'.

93.   Otley devotes three pages to describing the view from the summit of
Skiddaw. Tattersall (*The Lakes of England*, 1836, p.88) is more succinct and
devotes a paragraph to listing the places which may be seen: the Solway
Firth, and the mountains of Scotland . . . the towns of Workington,
Maryport, Allonby and Cockermouth, Carlisle and Dumfries; in Scotland
can be seen Mount Criffel in Kirkcudbrightshire, and the island of
Hasten, the Bay of Wigton and the mouth of the Dee, the Bay of Glenluce
and occasionally the Mull of Galloway. The Ruskins were indeed fortu-
nate with the weather and visibility on the day they made the ascent of
Skiddaw. Ingleborough is approximately 45 miles from Skiddaw.

94.   Having completed their stay in Keswick, they drove out of the town on
the Penrith road, with Saddleback on their left. Grassmoor (2791 feet) lay
directly behind them some 10 miles away between Derwentwater and
Crummock Water. Helvellyn was 7 miles due south of them, with Shap
Fell some 16 miles away to the south east, half right as they looked out of
the carriage window. Half way between Keswick and Penrith they turned
right and followed a southerly route through Troutbeck (*not* the Troutbeck near Windermere), leaving Great Mell Fell on their left. As they
drove through Matterdale Helvellyn would have been on their half right
about 5½ miles distant. A couple of miles after Matterdale the road drops
down to the shore of Ullswater. The second largest lake in the district,

Ullswater is a little over 8 miles in length and less than a mile wide.

95. They evidently left the carriage at the point where their road joined the road which runs along the side of the lake, and walked the quarter mile along the lake to Lyulph's Tower. A small gothic house, Lyulph's Tower was built as a hunting lodge before 1783 by a Duke of Norfolk. In 1830 it was the 'lake residence' of the Hon. Henry Howard, M.P., of Greystoke.

   Curiously, the Ruskins do not appear to have planned this part of the tour with their usual thoroughness. Between their carriage and Lyulph's Tower is the short footpath which would have taken them to Aira Force, a picturesque waterfall in Gowbarrow Park. This omission perhaps points to the fact that they were using Otley's *Guide*, for although he devotes seven lines to the Force in his section on Waterfalls, it is only mentioned in passing in the body of the *Guide*, and is not marked on the map. It is strange that they also failed to observe that it was here, on the edge of Ullswater below Gowbarrow Park, that Wordsworth is reputed to have 'wandered lonely as a cloud' in 1804 and seen his daffodils.

96. Patterdale Hall was at this time referred to as the Palace because it had formerly been the home of the Mounsey family. The Mounseys had been known as the kings of Patterdale since an early representative of the family, heading a group of local peasants, had defeated a group of marauding Scotsmen at Stybarrow Crag. By 1830 Mr Mounsey had sold the Hall to William Marshall, M.P., moving himself a couple of miles up the valley to Goldrill Cottage.

97. Parsons & White (op. cit.) list two inns in Patterdale in 1829, the King's Arms (Mary Dobson) and the White Lion (William Grave). The White Lion is a small inn and it was probably at the King's Arms where the Ruskins stayed. The name of the inn was changed to the Patterdale Hotel about the middle of the last century when the process of enlargement began.

98. Having enthused in *Iteriad* about the 'fine potted char' which they had for dinner, Ruskin then recorded that they went for a walk afterwards. First they found a huge dirty dunghill behind the inn, and a dirty duck and her ducklings on a puddle, then they ascended a 'small molehill' some fifty feet high. Having retraced their steps to the inn because it began to rain, they later made another excursion to the banks of the lake.

99. The route from Patterdale lay past Brothers Water and over Kirkstone Pass, to Ambleside, and on to Low Wood, a distance of 10 miles. The Ruskins were clearly displeased at having to take four horses instead of their usual two for this part of the journey. *Iteriad* records:

> We were just about to set off for Low Wood
> When up hopped a red-haired and sour-looking maid
> Who made bold to tell us, now guess what she said, –
> Why, that such a huge hill lay directly before,
> We must somehow contrive to take two horses more.

The actual ascent of Kirkstone from the Patterdale side is about 1 ¾ miles long with gradients ranging from 12 per cent to 25 per cent. Tattersall (op. cit.) observed that the pass 'is the steepest carriage road in the region of the Lakes', while Otley (op. cit.) who described the drive in the opposite direction, said 'This is a very steep carriage road, rising to 1300 feet above Ambleside, and falling to 900 feet on the other side.' John Robinson, writing in his *Guide* a few years earlier, had described Kirkstone as 'truly an alpine pass with high and naked mountains'. I can find no guide book writer who actually recommends the number of horses required for the pass. It is clear from Ruskin's account that once they had reached the top of the pass – there was no Kirkstone Pass Inn at that time – they dispensed with the services of the extra pair of horses which would have then returned to Patterdale. The descent into Ambleside is as steep as the ascent but longer and more tortuous.

100.   They were evidently well pleased to be back at Low Wood ('And we, very happily, took up our quarters'), and were made welcome on their return:

> Bobbed out Mrs Jackson with 'How d'ye do, sir?
> I hopes you're quite well; and miss, madam, and you, sir
> Your beds are well aired, and your rooms are all ready,
> These horses are troublesome; – steady, Jack, steady!'

We know from Book I of *Iteriad* that the Ruskins had warned the Jacksons ten days earlier of their intended return:

> And so that our beds might not want a good warming
> To our host, of our coming again we gave warning.

101.   Rydal Chapel was about 3 miles north of Low Wood, through Ambleside on the Grasmere road. It had been built in 1824 by Lady Ann Fredicia Elizabeth le Fleming at a cost of £1500. At this time the incumbent was the Revd Fletcher Fleming. Rydal Hall, nearby, had been the ancestral home of the le Fleming family since the time of Henry VI. Lady Fleming's husband had recently died. Her son, The Revd Sir Richard Fleming, was rector of Grasmere.

102.   William Wordsworth lived at this time at Rydal Mount, to which he had moved in 1813 and where he died in 1850. He had been appointed Distributor of Stamps for Westmorland about 1813, a post which he occupied until 1842. At the time of Ruskin's visit to Rydal Chapel, Wordsworth was in fact sixty years of age, and was between his 1829 visit to Ireland and the 1831 visit to Scotland and Sir Walter Scott at Abbotsford. Ruskin and his father eventually met Wordsworth at Oxford in 1839 when Ruskin won the Newdigate Prize for Poetry and Wordsworth was given an honorary degree. Wordsworth was appointed Poet Laureate in 1843.

103.   Possibly Thomas Wilkinson (?1751–1836), a friend of Wordsworth who featured in the latter's 'To the Spade of a Friend'.

104.   The circular house on Belle Island was designed by John Plaw for a Mr English and built in 1774. The partly completed mansion was bought in 1781 by Miss Isabella Curwen, and it passed from her to her husband J. C. Curwen. In 1830 Belle Island, the largest island in the lake, and the house, belonged to H. C. Curwen. Otley said that the house was encircled by a gravel walk of nearly two miles length 'which strangers are freely permitted to perambulate'.

105.   The Ferry Inn is on the west, or Lancashire, side of Windermere. The station is a tower on the hill just behind the inn.

106.   Rowing and sailing on Windermere had been popular long before the establishment of the Royal Windermere Sailing Club, and many formal and informal regattas and races were held over the years. In 1830 the

official Windermere Regatta was held on 3 September, starting from Low Wood. Perhaps the race the Ruskins saw was a practice for the regatta later in the year.

107. On this day, their route down the side of Windermere by carriage through Bowness to the ferry would have followed the way they had rowed home from Bowness on the previous day. A ferry service had been operated at this, the narrowest point on Windermere, since at least 1454. In 1830 the ferry rights were owned by the Curwen family and the service was operated by the Ferry Inn. Until 1869 when the first steam ferry was introduced, the boats were large flat-bottomed craft operated by oars. In *Iteriad* Ruskin wrote of the ferry:

> That the waters may not bar the path of the rover,
> A kind of hobblety boat paddles over;
> And, in order to urge on its clumsiness fast,
> They've got a huge oar that might do for a mast:
> And, what is much worse, they have not got a sail,
> That might catch in its foldings the breath of the gale.

Apparently the ferryman 'demanded and asked an exorbitant price'.

108. From the landing point on the western shore of Windermere their route lay through Far and Near Sawrey, past Esthwaite on the left, through Hawkshead, turning left by Hawkshead Hall and climbing the long steep Hawkshead Hill. From Hollin Bank they would have had a view of almost the entire length of Coniston Lake, had it not been obscured by the rain which by now was falling. From here to the Waterhead Inn at the head of Coniston Lake is about a mile, a total distance of about 7 miles from the ferry.

In 1830 the Waterhead Inn was situated in a field at the head of the lake. It probably began life as a farm house. In 1819 it was called the New Inn, to distinguish it from the Black Bull in Coniston village. In 1830 the landlord was William Cowbourn. It was a favourite inn with the Ruskins who visited it on more than one occasion. It was destroyed by fire about 1860 and the new Waterhead Hotel, which replaced it, was built between the road and the lake side, nearer to Coniston. In 1867 Ruskin wrote to his mother (*Bem* B VI) 'Our old Waterhead Inn, where I was so happy playing in the boats, *exists* no more. Its place is grown over with smooth park grass . . .'.

109. Ruskin's statistics are wrong here. Coniston Old Man is 2633 feet high. Forty one years later Ruskin was to buy a house, Brantwood, on the eastern shore of Coniston Lake, opposite the Old Man, and make it his home for the remainder of his life. He died there in 1900 and was buried in Coniston Churchyard. In 1933 Brantwood was opened as an international memorial to Ruskin and remains open to the public today.

110. Ruskin frequently waxed ecstatic about food in *Iteriad*. In the case of lunch at the Waterhead Inn, Coniston, he wrote (Book IV, lines 543ff.)

> We were monstrously hungry; so do not you marvel
> That we did not take time nor attempt for to carve well
> So went to the business at once, and indeed
> For capital carving there wasn't much need;
> So declared with the viands immediate war
> And dined upon taties and fine potted char.

The char (*Salmo Willugbii*) is a lake fish which thrives best in still, deep waters of low temperature. It resembles the trout in appearance but is more gorgeous in colour. The char is found in many lakes in Great Britain, but the fish vary greatly in their habits in different waters. In the Lake District they are found in Windermere, Coniston, Haweswater, Gaites Water and Seathwaite Tarn. They average something under half a pound in weight and are about eight inches long. The char makes excellent eating and potted char is a well-known delicacy. It was featured as a speciality in the 1825 Low Wood advertisements, and is listed on the printed bill-head of the Royal Oak, Keswick, in the mid-nineteenth century. To prepare potted char, first cook the char in prepared vegetable stock and let them cool in the liquid. Remove all skin and bones and arrange the fillets of fish, well drained, in shallow earthenware pots. Cover with clarified butter and set in oven for quarter of an hour. Allow to get quite cold and add a few more spoons full of clarified butter, if necessary, so that the fish is completely covered. Potted char will keep for two weeks in a cool place and was often sent home as a present by nineteenth century Lakes tourists.

111.   In order to avoid the ferry and its high price, they returned by way of the main road through Skelwith Bridge and round the head of Windermere, to Ambleside and Low Wood, a distance of about 10 miles. This route was, in fact, about 2 miles shorter than the outward journey.

112.   They left Low Wood on Saturday 10 July and spent that night and the following at Bowness, 4 miles south of Low Wood. Where they stayed in Bowness is uncertain. John Ullock's White Lion (now the Royal Hotel) and The Stag's Head were the posting houses and where one might have expected them to stay. On the other hand in 1867 when he was staying at the Crown in Bowness (now Crown Court Flats, 100 yards from the church on the old Bowness–Newby Bridge road) Ruskin wrote to his mother (*Bem* B VI, 1 July) '[I] got a lovely little corner-parlour in, I believe, your old inn, though I am much confused about it, the view seeming to me so much more beautiful than it did then . . .'. The landlord of the Crown in 1830 was Robert Aitkin. Both the White Lion and the Stag are nearer to the church than the Crown.

113.   Biskey How, a vantage point behind the town.

114.   Newby Bridge is a further 7½ miles south, at the foot of the lake.

115.   The church of St Martin, Bowness, was originally built in the twelfth century and re-built about 1480. It was restored and enlarged between 1869 and 1873. The east window contains a large amount of early painted glass, dating from between 1260 and 1480, which may have been brought here from Cartmel Priory although at the time of Ruskin's visit it was thought that the glass had come from Furness Abbey. In 1830 the rector was The Revd Sir Richard Fleming, his kinsman, the Revd John Fleming officiating as his curate.

116.   Probably Fairbank, on the road to Staveley.

117.   The route from Bowness to Kendal may have been by way of Staveley, or they may have taken the scenically more attractive road through Crook. The distance by either route is about 9 miles.

118.   Kendal Castle, the ancient seat of the Barons of Kendal, was the birthplace of Katherine Parr, the last wife of Henry VIII. It was in ruins by the seventeenth century and is more interesting from a distance than it

is at close quarters.

119. They probably breakfasted at one of the two posting houses in the main street, the Green Dragon (Nicholas Harrison), or the Rose and Crown (Hannah Roper).

120. Writing in 1875 (*Fors Clavigera* Letter 52, *Works* XXVIII:298), Ruskin said that 'The valley of the Lune at Kirkby is one of the lovliest scenes in England – therefore, in the world. Whatever moorland hill, and sweet river, and English forest foliage can be at their best, is gathered there; and chiefly seen from the steep bank which falls to the stream side from the upper part of the town itself. There, a path leads from the churchyard out of which Turner made his drawing of the valley . . .'.

121. Perhaps the first record of Devil's Bridge at Kirkby Lonsdale was in 1275 when it was repaired. The present old bridge is constructed of white freestone and at one end is a stone dated 1633. The three semi-circular arches span 51 feet and are supported by massive piers. Since Ruskin's visit traffic has been diverted onto an adjacent, newer bridge.

122. Where they joined their northbound route.

123. The Race Meeting on Preston Moor was established in 1726 and continued with a few breaks until 1786. In that year a rival meeting was established on Fulwood Moor, on the north-eastern outskirts of Preston. Thereafter the new meeting flourished and the former one seems to have stopped. Racing continued at Fulwood, under the name of Preston Races, until 1833. Thereafter there was a break of nine years before the meeting was revived. It finally finished in 1848.

124. Edward Smith Stanley, twelfth Earl of Derby, whose principal seat was at Knowsley, near Liverpool. Lord Derby had long taken an active interest in Preston Races and it was largely because of him that the Fulwood Meeting was established. Many generations of Stanleys had been members of Parliament for Preston. In 1830 the member was Edward George Geoffrey Smith Stanley, who was to become the fourteenth earl.

125. The Standish Arms (Elizabeth Hyde), Yarrow Bridge, Duxbury.

126. At this stage they were re-tracing the route of the outward journey. At Disley they may have breakfasted at the Ram's Head in Fountain Square.

127. From Chapel-en-le-Frith to Castleton is about 5½ miles. In Castleton they probably put up at the Castle Inn, the principal hotel in the village, which has three bow windows. The landlady in 1830 was Mrs Margaret Wragg.

128. With his interest in geology, Ruskin must have been eagerly looking forward to the visit to Castleton with its caverns and interesting geological formations. The party would have found the path to the Peak Cavern, almost immediately behind the inn and on their way to the entrance they would have walked through the oldest part of Castleton, with its old lead miners' cottages in the entrance to the gorge. At the time of the Ruskins' visit, rope making was carried on in the entrance to the Cavern and the rope makers' cottages were actually built within the entrance. Rope making here stopped when the last active rope maker retired in 1974. This is the point at which today's visitor is admitted to the Cavern, although in 1830 the admission point was a little farther in, at the point where they passed through the 'small door' and actually lost all daylight. The Cavern today is still much the same as described by Ruskin. To make things easier for the visitor, a new tunnel has been cut to bypass the 'little river Styx' and the necessity for the short boat trip. The caves are now lit

by electricity and so the guides can now display the glories of nature without recourse to candles and Bengal lights.

129. This point at the back of the entrance hall is now guarded by a gate. Clearly there was a door there in Ruskin's time in order to increase the impact of returning to natural light. From this point onwards one can also feel the atmosphere increasing in temperature, from the constant 47°F of the Cavern

130. It has not been possible to trace this Visitors' Book.

131. The entrance to the Speedwell Cavern (as it is now known) is at the foot of Winnats Pass, half a mile due west of Castleton village. Strictly speaking, Speedwell is a mine rather than a natural cavern. The half mile long tunnel was cut through solid limestone between 1774 and 1781, but unfortunately it was found to be poor in lead ore. The canal is some 70 feet below ground and visitors are still transported by boat. Ruskin's tremendous unfathomable gulph is today known as 'The Bottomless Pit', some 40,000 tons of rubble having been dumped here by the original miners without affecting the water level. The height of the roof above 'The Bottomless Pit' has still not been measured. It curves out of sight after 140 feet, and may be 300 feet high. The account describes the mine as 'the most horrible' of all the horrible places they had ever been in, and remembering the event when writing *Praeterita* (*Works* XXXV:75–6) Ruskin wrote: '. . . I pursued by mineralogical studies on fluor, calcite, and the ores of lead, with indescribable rapture when I was allowed to go into a cave. My father and mother showed far more kindness than I knew, in yielding to my subterranean passion; for my mother could not bear dirty places, and my father had a nervous feeling that the ladders would break, or the roof fall in, before we got out again. They went with me, nevertheless, wherever I wanted to go, – my father even into the terrible Speedwell mine at Castleton, where, for once, I was a little frightened myself.'

132. Mam Tor (1700 feet) is the hill immediately on the right as one ascends Winnats Pass from the Speedwell Mine. The Ruskins would have been able to hire a chaise and horse from Mrs Wragg at the Castle Inn for the journey. There are many hollows on the hillside which have been scooped out by the action of the atmosphere on the siliceous shale and sandstone of which the hill is constructed. Exposure to the atmosphere causes the disintegration of the stone which trickles down to the valley below. Because of this movement Mam Tor has been called the 'Shivering Mountain'. The view from the top of Mam Tor is generally considered to be very fine.

133. The route from Castleton by way of the Hope Valley and Hathersage would have approached Sheffield through Abbeydale, where 47 years later, the Guild of St George, inspired and financed by Ruskin, was to buy a small estate. It was also in Sheffield where the first museum of the Guild of St George was established by Ruskin, and where the Guild collection is still housed. (see Hewison: *Art and Society; Ruskin in Sheffield 1876*, Guild of St George, 1981)

134. The firm of Joseph Rodgers & Sons is regarded as Sheffield's second oldest firm of cutlers. Their foundation can be traced back to 1682. They were taken over by another organization in 1968 and ceased trading under their own name soon after that date. William White's *Directory of*

Sheffield, (1833), gives their address as 6 Norfolk Street and describes them as 'King's cutlers, merchants, and mfrs of pen, pocket and table knives, silver and plated desserts, razors, and scissors; & silver plate &c.' The knife which Ruskin saw 'containing 1821 blades', now known as 'The Year Knife', is an incredible instrument. In 1821 John Rodgers was presented to the Prince Regent and in the following year the firm was appointed Cutlers to the King. To celebrate the royal meeting and appointment, and the opening of the first Joseph Rodgers showrooms in 1821, the Year Knife was made, with 1821 blades. It continued to have this number of blades until at least 1837. In 1851 the knife was exhibited at the Great Exhibition. At some date it was decided to add a blade each year and in 1968, when the firm was taken over, it is reported to have had 1968 blades. In 1969 a blade was added to celebrate the moon landing and another was added in 1977 to celebrate the Queen's Silver Jubilee. In 1969 the knife was sold at Sotheby's and bought by Stanley Works G.B. Ltd. They have exhibited it world-wide, and when not on its travels it has been shown in Sheffield, in the City Museum. I am indebted to Mr David Alston for this information. Ruskin was, of course, quite correct in referring to George IV as 'his late majesty' since he had died three weeks earlier, on 26 June, while the Ruskins were staying at Keswick. He was succeeded by his brother, William IV. I have been unable to trace the 'twelve pairs of scissors'.

135.   The present church at Hope replaced its original Saxon predecessor in the fourteenth century. There is some interesting glass, carvings and paintings. At the time of Ruskin's visit, the vicar of Hope was the Revd Francis Orton, who was the incumbent from 1829 until 1843.

   The extensive repairs to the church of St Edmund, Castleton, were undertaken during the early 1830s. The roof lead was relaid, a new south porch was built, and the chancel was much restored. There are no records of how long the work took to complete, but the lead hopper heads to the drain pipes are dated 1831. The vicar of Castleton at the time was the Revd Charles Cecil Bates. He was the incumbent from 1817 until 1853 and the east window was later given in his memory.

136.   Little is known of William Peverel to whom William I granted the manor of Castleton, although Sir Walter Scott's *Peveril of the Peak* is a novel about him and his family. Ruskin was later to own the manuscript of this novel. Few castles have such a fine natural protection as Peveril or Peak Castle on its hill above the village which grew as an appendage to it. Most of the present castle dates from 1176, after the time of the Peverels. The castle was given by Edward III to John of Gaunt, Duke of Lancaster, and it remains in the possession of the Duchy of Lancaster today. It was a ruin by the early sixteenth century.

137.   This reference is obscure. Presumably Sir Walter Scott's son was staying in the village at the time of the Ruskins' visit. Scott had two sons, Walter (b. 1801) and Charles (b. 1805).

138.   I am unable to trace reference to a Bradshaw Mine. Ruskin has probably mis-heard or mis-remembered the name and is probably referring to the Bagshawe Cavern at Bradwell. Bradwell is two miles south-east of Castleton by the Tideswell road, or three miles by taking the road south from Hope. The Bagshawe Cavern, one of the most curious of the Derbyshire caverns, was accidentally discovered by lead miners in 1807.

Glover's *Peak Guide*, 1830, says '. . . A hundred and twenty six perpendicular and irregular steps conduct the visitor to a natural rotunda, with a small opening in the roof, through which the miners first descended by means of a chain . . .'. It is evident from Ruskin's description that they never penetrated as far as the 'Grotto of Paradise' with the arches of its roof 'pointed like those of a gothic hall'. The floor is formed of black and white spar producing an interesting chequered effect.

139.   Their route from Castleton probably lay by way of Hope to Hathersage, where turning right they would have gone on via Froggatt to Bakewell. The journey on from Bakewell to the New Bath Hotel at Matlock was another 9½ miles, so they would have been hungry by the time they ate their dinner. They had already stayed here for a number of days on their outward journey in June.

140.   The 'friend' is unidentified.

141.   Perhaps at Bakewell they breakfasted at the Rutland Arms Hotel, where about 30 years later the cook, by mistake, made the first 'Bakewell Pudding'. They no doubt stopped to look at the church which dominates the town, though it clearly did not make as much impression on Ruskin in 1830 as it did when he re-visited Bakewell in 1875, and wrote in his diary (*Bem* MS 19, 81; Evans & Whitehouse: *The Diaries of John Ruskin*, 836): 'The Norman west door at Bakewell is an intensely interesting example from its crude and savage variety, but the church entirely spoiled by horrible modern manufactured Gothic south transept door . . .'. The west front and door were built in 1160.

142.   Unidentified. Ruskin is evidently referring to a place which he thought was called Stoness – which I cannot find on the map – as opposed to visiting the home of people called Stones, because the long 's' has been employed for the first of the double 'ss'. Had Ruskin meant 'Stone's [house]', the long 's' would not have been employed.

143.   Ruskin does not record where they breakfasted. Perhaps they went to the Green Man and Black's Head in the main street, or one of the several inns which border the market place.

144.   While not being a cathedral, Ashbourne Church is certainly large and imposing. Dedicated to St Oswald, the present building was consecrated in 1241 and it was described by George Eliot as 'the finest mere parish church in the kingdom'. Among the examples of modern glass, probably not there in 1830, is the story of David and Goliath. An anecdote is recorded in the *St James's Gazette*, 23 January 1900, of Ruskin visiting the church in 1875–6 and being appalled at the 'ghastly daub' which 'would disgrace a penny edition of Jack the Giant Killer'. Anyone seeing the window could only agree with Ruskin!

145.   The monument to Penelope, the six-year-old daughter of Sir Brooke and Lady Susannah Boothby was executed by Thomas Banks. The epitaph reads: 'She was in form and intellect most exquisite. The unfortunate parents ventured their all on this frail bark, and the wreck was total'.

146.   I cannot explain this interpolation.

147.   Ashbourne to Bromsgrove by this route is about 62 miles; the additional 14 miles from Matlock to Ashbourne brings the day's journey to 76 miles.

148.   The 1830 Parliamentary election at Evesham began on 2 August and continued until 4 August. Sir Charles Cockerell polled 231 votes and Archibald Lord Kennedy 148 votes; they were returned to the first

parliament of William IV. Of the 301 electors who voted, 107 were inhabitants of Evesham and 159 were not. As a result of the conduct of the election a petition was presented to parliament in November 1830 and the election was finally declared void. (G. May: *History of Evesham*, 1834)

149.   The route to Cheltenham from Bromsgrove via Evesham would have been 37 miles, but having to take the alternative route added another 11 miles to the journey.

At this time Cheltenham was a fashionable and flourishing town, a popularity which it owed to the discovery there a few years earlier of a number of springs or wells of water said to have medical properties. During the second half of the century the continental spas gained popularity and Cheltenham declined, becoming a popular town for retirement from India and the army. Ruskin was here again in 1851 and in 1884 he wrote to Joan Severn from Farnley Hall, after leaving the town, 'If only Cheltenham had been an endurable place . . . But it was too horrid. The contrast between its vulgarity, inside and out, and this grand old hall is something marvellous . . .'. (13 December 1884, *Bem* L 36, quoted in *Works* XXXVII:501–2)

In 1830, the weekly *Cheltenham Journal* of 9 August recorded the arrival in the town of 'Mr Reaskin'.

The Plough in the High Street was a substantial hotel 'long frequented by the first families in the kingdom' which 'has fully kept pace with the increasing opulence of the town'. The landlord in 1830 was probably a Mr Naylor, but John Churchill took over from him about this time. The hotel was demolished in 1983 to make way for redevelopment, but the facade onto the High Street has been reconstructed. The lodgings which the Ruskins took across the road from the Plough were at No. 109 High Street, on the corner of Winchcombe Street. The house was occupied by Mr Alder, a chemist and druggist, and it was quite usual during the early nineteenth century for many of the rooms above the High Street shops to be let as lodgings during the summer. The High Street was re-numbered about 1957, no. 109 becoming 159. The ground floor is now occupied by a boutique, 'Chelsea Girl' and has a modern shop window, but the facade above is original, the first floor windows still retaining the iron balconies.

150.   Montpellier Gardens are at the opposite end of The Promenade to the High Street. Montpellier Spa was established by H. Thompson in 1809 and developed by his son, Pearson Thompson, who owned the property in 1830. By this time he had enlarged the original Pump Rooms, and had also built the Great Rotunda, which was finished in 1826. Associated with the establishment were reading rooms, a card room, and walks, rides and drives. The Rotunda is 50 feet in diameter and 54 feet high. Williams's *New Guide to Cheltenham*, (1828), explains that 'between six and seven [in the morning] the walks begin to be filled, and from seven till nine they are crowded'.

151.   The Royal Well was the original Cheltenham Spa. It was discovered by a Mr Mason who sold the waters for their medical properties between 1718 and 1721. The spa was developed in 1738 by Capt. Henry Skillicorne. He built the Old Pump Room and laid out the Upper and Lower Well Walks and planted the avenue of poplars which feature in many engravings of

the period. The square arched building had been built to shelter a pump, but by 1830 the pump had been removed and the well closed down. When the Ruskins were there The Royal Well belonged to the Revd Nash Skillicorne who had rented it to Capt. Matthews, who in turn re-let it to Mr Chambers. Williams's *New Guide* does not refer to the aviary.

152.   The Sherborne Spa was opened in 1818 and was on the site now occupied by the Queen's Hotel. The Promenade was laid out as the half mile long approach road to the spa. The Pump Room has a 100 feet long portico supported by six 20 feet high Ionic columns with a fine dome over its centre.

153.   Pittville is on the opposite side of the High Street to the other spas. In 1824 Joseph Pitt sold about a hundred acres for development as a new suburb, with certain restrictions. His plan included a Pump Room, lawns, shrubberies, rides, drives and promenades. The first stone of the Pittville Pump Room was laid by Mr Pitt on 4 May 1825, and it was opened for the first time on 20 July 1830 – in fact on the second day of the Ruskins' stay at Matlock. The Pittville Pump Room is one of the town's finest buildings, with its colonnades, pillars, statues, and seventy feet high dome. The direct approach to Pittville is along Winchcombe Street, on the corner of which the Ruskins had taken lodgings. On 5 August the name of 'Mr Ruskin and family, 109 High Street' was entered into the Pittville Spa Subscription Book (now belonging to the Cheltenham Local Studies Library and on permanent loan to the Pittville Pump Room Museum) showing that he had paid four shillings, entitling him and his family to walk in Pittville Park for one month. He did not subscribe for the waters, nor to ride or drive in the Park.

154.   William Frederick, second Duke of Gloucester (1776–1834) had married his cousin Mary, fourth daughter of George III and sister to William IV who had recently ascended to the throne on the death of his brother George IV on 26 June 1830. In August 1830 the Duke of Gloucester was staying in Cheltenham at 18 Royal Crescent. His name appears on 4 August 1830 in the Pittville Spa Subscription Book showing that he paid 2 guineas, a family subscription for the season. On 14 August they were visited for the day by the Duchess of Kent and her daughter the Princess Victoria. The occasion was recorded in the *Times* of 17 August 1830:

> Cheltenham Aug. 14. The Duchess of Kent and the Princess Victoria came over this morning from Malvern on a visit to the Duke of Gloucester. They arrived at his Royal Highness's residence, No. 18 [Royal] Crescent, a few minutes before one o'clock. Soon afterwards the Royal Duke, attended by his suite, and Mr Marshall, the Master of the Ceremonies, accompanied their Royal Highnesses to the Pump-rooms and other public buildings about the town. The Royal Party went first to the Old Well, where they stayed a few minutes, and then continued their progress to the Montpellier. The band of this Spa, in full uniform, struck up 'God Save the King', as the Royal Party entered the Promenade-room. The Duke of Gloucester conducted his relatives across the Rotunda towards the pump, and the Duchess and the young Princess both tasted the Spa waters. Their Royal Highnesses expressed [themselves] much pleased with the appearance and effect of the rooms, and the band, with continued playing during their

stay. They next crossed the road, and viewed the gardens which have recently been opened opposite the Rotunda. The carriages of the Royal Party conveyed them a short distance along the new Gloucester-road, in front of Lansdown-place; then, returning again, proceeded into the Pump-room at Pittville, where their Royal Highnesses alighted and remained a short time examining this magnificent building. The Duke of Gloucester conducted his illustrious visitors to the Assembly-rooms in the High Street, and to the Imperial or Sherbourne Spa, which latter place was tastefully decorated with festoons and flowers, and thence to the Duke's residence in the Crescent where the Duchess and Princess, it is expected, will dine with His Royal Highness, and in the evening return to Malvern. The bells in the old church rang a merry peal the whole of their Royal Highness' stay. The weather was very inauspicious, it rained incessantly, and the party was obliged to proceed from place to place in closed carriages. The Duke of Gloucester is one of the most regular water drinkers at the Montpellier Spa. The Princess Esterhazy is expected here in the course of a few days.

155.   Gloucester was a busy port, the Severn being navigable as far as the city. The last bridge over the Severn (before Bristol) crosses the river at the foot of Westgate Street. Cargoes of coal, lead, pig iron, grain and wool passed in and out of the port. There is no indication of the name of the inn to which they returned for lunch but perhaps it had been the Bell in Southgate Street, or the New Inn in Northgate Street.

156.   The Cathedral Close lies to the north of Westgate Street and is entered by way of King Edward's Gate. One can still not walk right round the cathedral, only around the west and south sides, gardens and other buildings preventing access to the other sides.

157.   Gloucester Cathedral has been described as the sixth most beautiful building in Europe. It stands on the site where the first monastery in Gloucester was founded in 681 A.D. Two earlier buildings were destroyed before the third monastery was re-founded in 1048. Abbot Serlo was sent to Gloucester by William I; work on the new abbey church began in 1089 and it was consecrated in 1100. Abbot Serlo destroyed the earlier Saxon church and the Norman pillars and arches of the nave are probably his work. The very elegant main tower (there is no steeple) replaced an earlier one which was taken down in 1450. The present tower is 225 feet high. Ruskin made a fine drawing of the cathedral tower in 1834.

158.   Ruskin was probably looking into Abbot Serlo's Norman crypt of 1089. Its massive pillars were later reinforced to carry the weight of the new Choir. The floor is about 8 feet below ground level and the centre aisle is divided by two rows of small piers, irregularly placed, from which spring round arches carrying the weight of the Choir above.

159.   They obviously entered the cathedral by the south porch, with its 800 years old original doors and hinges and walked round the cathedral in a clockwise direction. The 'Saxon' pillars are of course the original Norman pillars of 1089.

160.   Edward Jenner (1749–1823), the discoverer of vaccination, was born and died in the county. His statue stands in the south aisle.

161.   They had now passed the west door and were walking up the north aisle.

The monument to which Ruskin refers here is by Flaxman and comme-
morates Sarah Morley and her child who died at sea.

162.   Revelation XX, 13

163.   This is probably the seventeenth century monument in the north
transept, with a painted oak panel, depicting John Bower, his wife in a
Welsh hat, and their nine slender sons and seven devout daughters,
painted in perspective.

164.   These references are probably to the screens around the North and
South Ambulatory, with the Cenotaph of Abbot Parker, the tomb of
Edward II, the Chapel of St Edmund the Martyr, the Lady Chapel Bridge
and the Chapels of St Stephen and St Andrew.

165.   The guide's story seems to have been confused. There was a fire in 1300
which destroyed the domestic buildings, but not the Choir. Ruskin is
probably referring to the part of the cathedral, at the entrance to the
South Transept, where the Perpendicular work of the new Choir joins the
earlier Norman work. The arches and columns here are noticeably less
heavy and there are interesting flying arches carrying the springing of the
last division of the fourteenth century choir vault. This perpendicular
gothic work may be the earliest in the country. The new work here was
funded by the revenue from pilgrims to the tomb of Edward II following
his murder at Berkeley Castle and burial here in 1327.

166.   The guide was quite correct. At that time part of the crypt was used as a
Charnel House, as is illustrated in Plate XIII of J. Britton's *History and
Antiquities of Gloucester Cathedral*, (1829). In this plate, light from outside
may be seen shining on piles of skulls and larger bones.

167.   They probably left Cheltenham in the morning of Wednesday 18 August.
John James's itinerary shows that they returned to London by way of
Oxford and Langley. Cheltenham to Oxford is 40 miles and it seems
possible that they broke their return journey at the Angel at Oxford, as
they probably also did on the outward trip. This would have left the final
day's journey to Herne Hill of exactly the same duration as the first day of
their tour, 18 May. They would thus have arrived home on Thursday 19
August, having been away for three months.

Appendix I

Extract from a letter from John James Ruskin to John Ruskin, Preston, 8 March 1831[1]

I wish I could give you an account that could give you an idea of the astonishing railway travelling between Liverpool & Manchester. I went to see them start at 4 O'Clock near Livl. They first enter a Tunnel larger than the Thames Tunnel from a large yard walled in. I was standing at the Gate & two persons not passengers were debating in the way   The immense Gate Kept sliding out of one Side in the way the Diorama seems to move till it squeezed the two men together, & would have sliced them longways & sideways like a Cucumber Knife leaving their face & front & toes inside the premises & the back of their head, their hinderparts & heels outside the premises. They quickly saved themselves by a retreat. The outlet of the Tunnel is between two high Rocks cut right down for the Level of Railway so that hastening to the top of Rock I looked down on the Railway which is merely a Road of unusual Breadth of a Highway having two Iron Railways laid down like those you have seen with only four feet between. On one of these are 5

---

1 The original letter from which this is extracted is in the Ruskin Galleries at Bembridge School. (*Bem* L 3) Most of this extract was first printed in the *Bembridge School Newspaper*, Christmas Term, 1960; 12 offprints were produced. The letter next appeared in 1973 in *RFL*, 236–7.

carriages with each 4 low but beautifully made Iron Wheels fitted to Railway – each Carriage has a triple Body with Capacious Seats for 6 – that is 18 each – or 90 passengers   The 5 triple Carriages are chained together & preceded by a most beautiful little Steam Engine not much larger than a huge mortar & having much the appearance of a piece of Ordnance – behind it is a Car very much like old Neptunes in which are two Boys like Sailor Boys managing the Machinery: It sets off with a sharp rattling noise – its pace increases – a dense & immense Cloud of Smoke flys off at one side – till Bounce Phizz – crack off it goes like some infuriate Spirit or infernal Engine dragging at its tail 5 Machines, fifteen Coach Bodies, 90 people at the rate of 30 miles an hour – They & all their Luggage seem but as the papers at the tail of a Kite, so easily does this little Imp of an Engine seem to fly away with them. I do think you would be delighted to be one of the Passengers. I do believe we should scarcely be able to keep Mama from taking a Journey – . . .

Appendix II   Poems

The tour was not allowed to interrupt Ruskin's writing of poetry. The Juvenile Notebook listed by W. G. Collingwood as No. V contains four poems dated during the tour, and a fifth, 'Love', whose position in Book V indicates that it was almost certainly written between 11 July and 2 August. 'Haddon Hall' was almost certainly written in June–July. 'My Fishing Rod', while not written until 20 December, almost certainly drew its inspiration from an incident in the Lake District, perhaps brought to mind by the writing of 'The Ascent of Skiddaw', Book III of *Iteriad*, which Ruskin wrote between 28 November and 26 December.

The poems are printed here from the Cook and Wedderburn transcripts at Bembridge (*Bem* T 27–28), with the exception of 'Haddon Hall', which is re-printed from the *Library Edition*. With the exception of 'Haddon Hall', the poems are hitherto unpublished.

The poems are as follows:

The Day of Judgement	22 May–13 June	*Bem* T27
Haddon Hall	June–July	vv 1–2 published in *Poems* I:39. v 3 added in *Works* II:284. v 3 is also in *Bem* T 27
Revenge	11 July	*Bem* T 28
Despair	11 July	*Bem* T 28
Love	? July	*Bem* T 28
Creation	2 August	*Bem* T 28
My Fishing Rod	20 December	*Bem* T 27

THE DAY OF JUDGEMENT

1

The sky was of the hue of blood
The clouds were dark and dun
The slumbering fire on the tempest rode
And crimson was the sun
No night had been so horrible
No breeze had such a sound
For God was on the tempest blast
That parched the panting ground.

2

The billow threw a darkened foam
That was not of the snow
And raised a mournful murmuring moan
As if in deepest woe
Man gazed upon the bloody sky
And on the murky cloud
And felt the burning breeze sweep by
But thought not on his God.

3

'Twas midnight and the tempest blew
The moon looked ghastly pale
Like birds of night the dæmons flew
And screamed upon the gale
The earth it shook most dreadfully
And quaked for very fear
The moon became as red as blood
The parting hour is near

4

The stars fell trembling to the ground
And black became the sun
The earth in inward terror groaned
For lo her hour is come
When sounding o'er the mighty sea
And o'er the trembling earth

And silencing the thunders roll
The trumpet blast had birth

5

Then widely yawned the horrid grave
The sea gave up its dead
And from the now departing wave
The righteous raised his head
On that cloud there was a throne
And dazzling was its light
For the Lamb sat there in glory
Than departed suns more bright

6

Then softly swelled his soothing voice
As he spoke unto the bless'd
Ye righteous and upright rejoice
In everlasting rest
Then rose a heavenly strain
As they sung the works of God
And their unclean sinful souls
All redeemed by his blood

7

But then he spoke in thunder
Depart accursed to hell
The rocks were rent asunder
And the trembling mountains fell
The accursed in dire confusion driven
Fallen headlong from the skies
The lightnings hurled them from the heaven
To where flames eternal rise

8

They gnashed their teeth in agony
Blasphemed the holy name
For there the fiery billows rolled
Crowned with a crest of flame
The lake of liquid sulphur broke

In sheets of living fire
And beat against the burning rock
So horrible and dire

9

Around their heads the thunders break
The living lightnings play
While devils laugh exultingly
And walk the burning way
And mid those flames were hellish forms
The venomed vipers rise
They dart their forked fiery tongues
And flash their flaming eyes

10

But oh, how different the abode
Of those who loved their God
And who have washed their robes of snow
In Christ's all-saving blood
Their bosom now no sorrow knows
No scorching tears can spring
For ever freed from all their woes
They touch the sacred string

11

How loud their golden lyres resound
O'er which their fingers rove
They sing the Saviour's agonies
And God's eternal love
And midst them all the Saviour shone
With grace and love and peace
High on his bright eternal throne
The Sun of Righteousness

12

They need no sun except their God
Who ever gives them light
No gloom can pierce that blest abode
And banished is the night

Their state of joy shall know no end
As does the worldly bliss
And they shall sing for evermore
Their Saviour's Righteousness

HADDON HALL

I

Old halls, and old walls, –
    They are my great delight;
Rusty swords and rotten boards,
    And ivy black as night!
Hey, ruination and hey, desolation, –
But created to spoil the creation!

II

Dry ditch, old niche, –
    Besides, an oaken table;
On't the warriors ate,
From a pewter plate,
    As much as they were able!
Hey, ruination and hey, desolation, –
Only created to spoil the creation!

III

O'er the mossy walk we next did stalk
    Gently for fear of tumbling;
For in that case
You'd make a face,
    Besides a noble grumbling.
Hey, ruination and hey, desolation, –
Only created to spoil the creation!

REVENGE

An Indian sky was overhead
That lurid sky was burning red

A sullen breeze was on the sea
It breathes no whispering harmony
5 And nature silent waits the hour
That shall reduce the white man's pow'r
In a braky thorny wood
A miserable cottage stood
At its faintly blazing fire
10 A hag repeats her orgies dire
Round her the chiefs impatient stand
And all of Afric's sultry land
Each warrior prays to his idol god
Then draws his knife thirsting for blood
15 The venom in a bowl was laid
Each Afric in it dips his blade
While as they stood the red fire threw
A ghastly paly sinking hue
Now it rose in spreading light
20 Now it almost sinks to night
And now revived again it shone
Upon the damp and mossy stone
Then the warwhoop swelled on the midnight blast
Shrill dreadful and dismal the ocean it past
25 Forth to the work of blood they came
They eyeballs flashed a horrid flame
And the unsheathed and naked brand
Shone broad and lightened in their hand
On their sleeping masters come
30 Still and silent as the tomb
Swift and sure the midnight death
Stole away their dying breath
Gasping from their slumber broke
But to feel the dreadful stroke
35 But to see the streaming gore
But to sink to rise no more
High o'er the horrid scene of blood
Revenge upon the thunder rode
His eyeballs shone with dire delight
40 Gazing on the frightful sight
His falchion was keen and red
With the gore of murdered dead
And in his hand a spear he shook

Dire and malignant was his look
45 He smil'd as he thought on murders done
As he thought on their victims dying groan
As he thought on their panting gasping breath
On their eyes for ever closed in death
On their icy limbs convulsed and quivering
50 At the approach of murder shivering
On these he thought and smiled so grim
For these were sport and play to him
And then in thunder loud he spoke
The deathlike sentence then he broke
55 Murder it is my bloody bride
I drink the blood of those who died
My bridal bed shall be the tomb
And there amid eternal gloom
Upon a bloody corse I'll rest
60 Pillowed on its late panting breast
'Tis there I'll lie and wait the hour
Till I again shall try my power

DESPAIR

The sails were filled with a gentle breeze
And they joyful swept o'er the summer seas
The azure sky around them shone
The waves had glory not their own
5 The knight had been to foreign lands
Far from his true love dear
And oft amid his country's bands
He mournful thought of her
Lord Hubert was the warrior's name
10 A sound that was not strange to fame
But something weighed upon his breast
He knew not what the thought might be
But heavier on him still it pressed
As the shores of his country appeared on the sea
15 It was something within him a something of sorrow
That told him of mourning and madness tomorrow
But when his native home he found
He heard the revels joyful sound

He saw them drink the rich red wine
20   The blood of the luxuriant vine
Beguiling the delaying day
He heard them laughing merrily
And his own hall with revellers filled
His heart with sad forebodings chilled
25   And it is thus the knight he spoke
Is my Lady's promise broke
Hath she given her snowy hand
Thinking me dead in a foreign land
And who art thou again they said
30   Art thou the Knight we thought was dead
Yes. Often was thy love besought
And often did she answer nought
Until Lord William of Lorraine
Unto thy Lady's hand laid claim
35   Twas then worn out with woe and grief
She yielded to the gallant chief
Struck dumb the noble warrior stood
Back to his heart recoiled his blood
Pale pale as death his visage seemed
40   Of murder and revenge he dreamed
He seems to stand on reeling ground
He rolls his furious eyes around
Enraged with agonising woe
His countenance like newfall'n snow
45   With all the passions dire appress't
He sunk upon the strangers breast
And long in that sad swoon he lay
For when he sunk twas noon of day
And when he woke the sinking sun
50   His glorious race of light had run
Upon a couch the warrior lies
He knew it, 'twas his own
He looked around with wondering eyes
It was his native home
55   But who sits weeping by his side
It is his fair but faithless bride
The salt salt tears unceasing flow
And down her snowy cheeks they flow
All scorching burning as they rolled

60 Amongst her locks of flowing gold
    From that soft couch the knight arose
    Plunged deep in sorrows and in woes
    And raised his eyes to heaven
    And now he bent them to the ground
65 And now he wildly gazed around
    By burning anguish driven
    But when he saw the faithless maid
    He sunk to calmer woe
    But not a single word he said
70 And tears began to flow
    Then from the couch on which he lay
    The warrior rose full silently
    And from the halls he once had known
    The house he once had called his own
75 His dearest and his native home
    He bent his silent way
    And in a secret nook
    His own good falchion, keen he took
    And thus the warrior said
80 Now serve me well my gallant blade
    Thy edge the Saracen shall feel
    The false and faithless Infidel
    Thy master's heart is well nigh broke
    But still his arm can strike one stroke
85 And ere I breath my parting sigh
    One infidel at least shall die
    With that he kissed the shining blade
    Then in the scabbard placed
    Devoted now to sacred use
90 Consigned it to its rest
    Full slowly and full silently
    The knight pursued his way
    And from his dear and native shore
    The land he now may see no more
95 Across the watery waste
    Swift swift the warrior past
    Seeking that holy clime
    The sultry scorching Palestine
    Far as the eye could sweep
100 The wilderness did lie

Smooth desert as the deep
And now a tree was nigh
But the Saracen was there
Full gorgeous full gay
105   Flags fluttered not in air
For no cooling breezes play
And on the wild Arabian horse
Each Pagan musters all his force
The lightnings round their falchions play
110   More dazzling than the Lord of day
Eager to slay their Christian foes
Their turbaned in order rose
While on the scorching sand
The Christians armies stand
115   And on his warlike steed
The warlike Richard sate
And in his armoured hand
He held his bloody battle brand
His eye was fraught with fire
120   His countenance was dire
And dreadful to his foes
It was a wrathful lion roused to rage
For when his anger rose
The wrathful passions nothing could assuage
125   Then they gave the reins to the barbed steed
And forth to the battle sprung
The Saracens bent their bow
And the whistling arrows sung
Richard was drunk with the Pagans blood
130   Through the thick of the battle and slaughter he rode
Death is behind and fear before
For all who meet him are no more
Until encircled all around
His wrath still higher rose
135   And back on every side
Recoiled his flying foes
But still unceasingly
Their poisoned darts they pour
For death is on the wing
140   It is a steely show'r

But he must sink at last
His arm is tired with slaughter and with death
His strength is failing fast
And shorter pants his breath
145   The knight beheld his sinking Lord
And drew his polished sword
He waved it high. It cleft the air
An infidel was bleeding there
Another wave around his head
150   Another infidel is dead
Amongst the Saracens he sprung
At every bound is falchion sung
At every bound a Pagan fell
The indignant soul sunk deep in hell
155   A Pagan raised his falchion
Twas poisoned and twas keen
To lay his master low
Lord Huberts breast received the blow
He sunk, his sword deserts his hand
160   His eyes are closed in night
The blood is bubbling from his breast
And stains his armour bright
He thought upon his Ladylove
And thus the warrior spoke
165   I've lived for thee, I die for thee
My faithful heart is broke
That poisoned blow has laid me low
My heart still beats for thee
Then, Oh in thine own native halls
170   A moment think of me
He stopped for death prevents the word
He feels the poison of the sword
His eyelids close in calm repose
The warrior sinks to night
175   The spirit rejected its load of clay
Joyful it sprung on its airy way
The struggle is past it has learned to rejoice
And it praises its God with a heavenly voice
Its woes are forgotten its sorrows are o'er
180   And the soul of the warrior grieveth no more.

LOVE

The babe was laughing joyfully
Upon its mothers knee
His cheeks were like the newblown rose
His little heart no sorrow knows
5   His bright blue eye
Was like a little gem
The babe knew nought but joy
For what should trouble him
But something stole upon the babe
10   His cheek grew wan and pale
Until it was like the snow
His eye grew dim and dull
A blight hath seized the flow'r
Alas and in an hour
15   The bud shall be laid low
And daily daily wasted he
The poison sharp of death
Would still consume him inwardly
And weaken every breath
20   And now upon his lowly bed
The once fair boy is laid
No human art can raise him now
The mark of death is on his brow
And sinks he rapidly
25   And long his mother watched his couch
And long his pains allayed
Alas, alas, fully mournfully
She watched his dying bed
And oft unto her God she prayed
30   That he might spare her babe
But God is infinitely wise
And he had willed it otherwise
The baby long did waste away
Until its cheeks were cold as clay
35   And months of pain it had endured
Before its agonies were cured
Twas then without a struggling sigh
It tasted immortality
And all its woes and all its care

40   And sufferings were dispersed in air
       Far from this world the spirit fled
       And to its native heaven sped
       And borne upon the angels wing
       The happy soul began to sing
45   Where now, O world are all thy treasures
       Where now is all my earthly care
       Like thee, O world, a subtle air
       Tis now I taste the joys of heaven
       To thee, O nether world not given
50   Meanwhile its mother left below
       Drained to the dregs the cup of woe
       The corse was in the coffin placed
       Consigned to its eternal rest
       Twas lowered in the grave
55   And with a dread unearthly sound
       Rung on its lid the crumbling sound
       The grave, the dull cold grave
       Received the baby's corse.
       Earth to earth and dust to dust
60   The body moulders into clay
       The soul hath immortality
       And from that mournful time
       The mother wasted too
       She wandered sadly far away
65   And where and whither shall she go
       Alas, the mother does not know
       For fire is feeding on her brain
       Madness hath not released her from her woe
       She could not speak she could not pray
70   And comfort was a stranger to her breast
       And still she thought she saw
       Her baby's icy clay
       The phantom it was seen by night
       And it was seen by day
75   And still the corse was there
       Stretched out so stiff, stretched out so cold
       And with its cheeks so ghastly white
       The sad remains of one so fair
       And then she rolled her eyeballs wild
80   And gazed upon the bright expanse

That all around was thrown
And then it calmed her woes
For ah, she knew her darling child
Amongst the angels shone
85   The cup of woe is full
God has poured out his wrath
And she hath drunk the dregs of bitterness
And lays her down to die
The fire of Heaven is in her eye
90   She sees the distant realms of bliss
She feels a spark of happiness
And sees again her boy
The spirit is fled
From the mortal dust it is gone
95   It is gone to its God
It is washed in his blood
It stands before the throne
The breath of life no more
Shall animate the clay
100   The spirit is gone to a distant shore
The mother and her babe
United in the grave
They now shall part no more

CREATION

A FRAGMENT

Day had not dawned upon the world
Earth was not formed to day
But all in one vast chaos hurled
Promiscuously lay
Night ruled o'er all so dark and deep
Day pierced not yet the solitude
The solitude of drear eternal sleep
One boundless waste.
Let there be light
The accents sounded strange but full of power
As o'er the airy wilderness they past
And awed the circumfusing night

Then first sprang forth the day
Born from astonished night
Which trembling fled away
And the first morning cheered the wilderness
Again the almighty word
Sounds o'er the deep abyss
A murmur hoarse rose from the boiling waves
Distinct and terrible
No other sound was heard
Save as the mighty waters backward sweep
And boiling in their bonds invisible
A raging fretting deep
A waste and watery wilderness of waves
Back from the earth retreat

MY FISHING ROD

I bought a fishing rod and line
I thought they were extremely fine
And both of them I do opine
Did cost me Half a crown

2

Thought I the next time I go out
Without a particle of doubt
I shall bring home a dish of trout
Quite ready to be fried

3

So I a poor presuming wight
Determined that the fish should bite
And do exactly as I like
I ran towards the pool

4

But ah, alas, can I relate
The envious trick of angry fate
For as I bore my rod in state
A sad mishap befell

5

For not observing what things lay
Before me in my headlong way
A bush (O bushes vile) did stay
My rods forward career

6

And so the slender yielding end
(To slender things I'm not a friend)
Because it found it could not bend
Determined – it would break

7

So crack it went. With consternation
And with a monstrous turbulation
I saw this downright ruination
Of all my joyous hopes

8

But having mended it once more
Again rejoicing to the shore
I bent my footsteps as before
And threw my line clear in

9

And there I stood till wearied out
Without a bite of Perch or Trout
And I felt much disposed to pout
Because the fish were wise

10

And then I caught an animal
That was so hugeously small
That I in anger Pish did call
And threw my line again

11

A tree there overhung the stream
And dipped its pendant branches in

And when I gave my line that fling
I hooked it in the tree.

12

And when I pulled to get it free
That troublesome presuming tree
Held it so fast in spite of me
That crack it went in two

13

Half of it hangs suspended there
Merrily dangling in mid-air
Alas, the weakness of horse-hair
Who ever thought 'twould break so

14

So mournfully I marched home
My line suspended o'er the foam
And with a fish as good as none
Certainly little better.

Index

Printed in Great Britain by
Dotesios Printers Ltd, Trowbridge, Wiltshire